K

100
FAMILIES

Who Shaped World History

Samuel Willard Crompton

A Bluewood Book

This edition produced and published
by Bluewood Books
A Division of The Siyeh Group, Inc.,
P.O. Box 689
San Mateo, CA 94401

ISBN 0-912517-34-4

Printed in U.S.A.
10, 9, 8, 7, 6, 5, 4, 3, 2, 1

Editor: Tony Napoli
Assistant Editor: Barbara King
Indexer: Kathy Paparchontis
Designer: Kevin Harris

Key to cover illustration:
    Clockwise, starting from top
left: Queen Victoria, Genghis
Khan, Louis XIV, Henry and Edsel
Ford, John Adams, FDR Crest
and Henry VIII in the center.

About the Author:
Samuel Willard Crompton
lives in western Massachusetts, where
he teaches American and European
history at Holyoke Community
College. Crompton is the author of
several books including: *100
Colonial Leaders Who Shaped North
America* (Bluewood, 1999), *100
Americans Who Shaped American
History* (Bluewood, 1999), *100
Battles That Shaped World History*
(Bluewood, 1997), *100 Military
Leaders Who Shaped World History*
(Bluewood, 1999), *100 Wars That
Shaped World History* (Bluewood,
1997). He is also the editor of the
*Illustrated Atlas of Native American
History* (Chartwell Books, 1999).
Crompton holds degrees from Duke
University and Framingham State
College.

Picture Acknowledgements:
Bluewood Archives: all pages except:
Archives of Canada: 69; British
Council: 35; British Airways: 67;
Embassay of India: 73; Ford Motor
Company: 43; German Informatrion
Center: 51; Guggenheim Foundation:
52; Harvard Univ. Library: 39;
Hawaii State Archives: 61; Monaco
Information Bureau: 49; JFK Library:
63; Library of Congress: 9, 18, 26,
33, 34, 36, 41, 46, 59, 68; Lowell
Observatory: 71; Mayo Clinic: 74;
Museum of the City of New York: 14;
National Archives: 38, 50, 76, 87;
National Gallery, London: 15;
Nebraska State Historical Society:
65; NYPL: 12, 22, 23, 37, 53, 90,
91, 97, 98; San Mateo Public
Library: 10, 16, 21, 32, 40, 45, 80,
93; Universal Pictures: 42; U.S.
Army: 31, 81; The White House: 25

TABLE OF CONTENTS

TABLE OF CONTENTS

TABLE OF CONTENTS

TABLE OF CONTENTS

INTRODUCTION

France justly boasts the Ancient Noble Line
Of Bourbon, Mommorency, and Lorrain.
The Germans too their House of Austria show,
And Holland their Invincible Nassau.

Daniel Defoe sang the praises of family dynasties in his poem *The True-Born Englishman* (1701). Many of the families described in this book fall within that category. The Abbasids of Baghdad, the Spanish and Austrian Hapsburgs, the Meiji of Japan, the Ming of China, and numerous other royal families boasted ancient lineages that entitled them to occupy thrones and rule great nations. These families claimed their rights by birth, and some of them lived up to the promise of their heritages, while others did not.

Defoe went on to poke fun at his own country of England, which contained almost no "true-born" nobles and lords; nearly all of them were descended from nobility of other countries. The Stuarts who ruled England from 1603 until 1775 were actually Scottish; they were succeeded by the House of Hanover, which originated in Germany, or the Holy Roman Empire, as it was then called. Defoe also accurately depicted the fact that England was turning into a nation that valued wealth above everything else; if one had wealth, but not a title, the title could be found to fit the fortune. This became especially true in England during the 1770s, after the beginning of the Industrial Revolution.

Revolutionary movements in Europe during the 17th and 18th century—culminating in the French Revolution in 1789— proclaimed the coming era of the common man, and by extension the era of the common family. In the 20th century, the Russian Revolution of 1917 and the defeat of Germany and the empire of Austria-Hungary in World War I the next year swept away many notable family dynasties forever.

By that time within the United States the pattern of "self-made" families had emerged. America had no titled aristocracy, and that allowed ambitious men and women who came from poor or very modest beginnings to achieve great wealth and success. John Jacob Astor started in America as a small-time fur trader; Cornelius Vanderbuilt was the son of a poor Staten Island, New York farmer and ferryman; Henry Ford began his working life as a mechanic. Yet, Astor's grandchildren ruled a vast real estate empire, and Vanderbuilt's heirs became titans of the railroad industry, as well as noted bankers and yachtsmen. Henry Ford parlayed his skills as a mechanic, became an engineer, and became the founder of the American automobile industry.

Of course, any book that only describes the family histories of the noble and wealthy class, would be neglecting the fascinating stories of those families who have made notable contributions in all walks of life. So, in the pages that follow, you will find stories about scientific families such as Bernoulli, Darwin, and Curie; stories about artistic families such as Bach, Barrymore, and Tolstoy; stories about political families such as Adams, Harrison, and Kennedy, as well as stories about the families that gave the world well-known explorers, military leaders, religious leaders, and even athletes.

The 100 families that comprise this book are a diverse lot—geographically, nationally, ethnically, and socially—and their lives stretch from the time of Alexander the Great up to the present day. Yet with all their diversity, these families do share a common trait: an astonishing vitality that somehow becomes "bottled" and passed down from generation to generation. How this happens remains something of a mystery—one that historians and sociologists can ponder for as long as families exist and endure.

1. Abbasid
Arabian caliphs

As the rulers of Baghdad and the Arabian empire, the **Abbasid** family presided as caliphs (supreme rulers) over the height of Arab civilization. The caliph was the director of both the spiritual and the worldly affairs of the empire, which stretched from **Spain** to **Baghdad** (present-day Iraq).

During the A.D.740s, the Abbasid family created an organization centered in Khurasan, a part of **Persia**. The family members claimed they were descendants of al-Abbas, the uncle of **Mohammed**, founder of **Islam**. Therefore, they asserted, they were the true heirs to his glory and the true leaders of the Arab world. With this claim, they challenged the rulers of the Arab empire at that time—the Umayyad dynasty.

In A.D.750, the Abbasids led a loose-knit coalition of Persians and Iraqis in a revolution against the Umayyads. The Abbasids won the key battle at the Great Zeb, a tributary of the **Tigris River**. The last Umayyad caliph was slain after he fled to Egypt.

Abu al-'Abbas al-Saffah, leader of the Abbasids, (reigned A.D.750-754), established his rule in the ancient city of Baghdad.

Known as "the Bloodshedder," he was an effective and feared conqueror of lands to the east. He was succeeded by his brother al-Mansur, who reigned from A.D.754 until A.D.775.

The Abbasid caliphate flourished during the reign of Harun al-Rashid (A.D.786–809). Al-Rashid presided over an explosion of learning in Baghdad, as the Arab court scholars translated the writings of Euclid, Galen, Ptolemy, Aristotle, Plato, and other Greek scholars into Arabic. Arab medicine achieved great prominence during this period, and the best scientists of the day flocked to Baghdad.

The reign of al-Mamun (A.D. 813–833), the son of al-Rashid, was probably the most glorious period in the history of the dynasty. Al Mamun established the **House of Wisdom** in Baghdad, a combination of an academy, library, and bureau of translations, where great literary, philosophical, and scientific works were translated. His brother and heir, al-Mu'tasim (reigned A.D. 833–842), moved the capital to **Samarra**, 100 miles north of Baghdad on the Tigris River. Al-Mu'tasim also took the fateful step of employing former Turkish slaves and mercenaries as bodyguards.

View of Baghdad

Within one generation, the guards assumed the real power and the caliphs became merely figureheads. Baghdad became the capital again in A.D. 883, but the Abbasid family never regained true authority.

The family continued to rule the Arab world in name, until 1258, when al-Musta'sim, the last Abbasid caliph, was executed by the soldiers of Mongke Khan, grandson of Genghis Khan. The Abbasids had held the caliphate from A.D. 750 until 1258, and 37 family members had held the title, though not necessarily the power, of caliph.

The contributions of the **Adams** family of Massachusetts, have seldom been equaled in American political life. If the young United States of America had a "royal" family, it was surely the Adamses.

The origins of the family began in England. There, Henry Adams married Edith Squire in 1609. The couple emigrated to the **Massachusetts Bay Colony** in 1636 and settled in Braintree, on the east coast of Massachusetts. The family produced solid if unremarkable citizens, until the 18th century, when **John Adams** and his second cousin, **Samuel Adams**, were born.

John Adams (1735–1826) yearned to be a soldier, but he was educated to be a lawyer. He served as defense counsel for the British soldiers implicated in the **Boston Massacre** of 1770. His strong patriotism propelled him into political affairs, and he served in the First **Continental Congress** and was one of the signatories of the Declaration of Independence.

Later, he served as vice president under George Washington, and then became the second U.S. president, serving from 1797 to 1801. As president, Adams became unpopular for his stand on the undeclared naval war with France in 1799; however, he left office convinced he had played his role correctly. Although Adams and **Thomas Jefferson** had been political foes, they reconciled and corresponded with each other in retirement. By a remarkable coincidence, the two men died within hours of each other on July 4, 1826, the 50th anniversary of the signing of the Declaration of Independence.

John's cousin, Samuel Adams (1722–1803), was a fiery speaker. He used his gifts of oratory to incite Boston crowds to action in incidents such as the **Boston Tea Party** in 1773. He was also a signatory of the

John Q. Adams

Declaration of Independence and served as lieutenant governor and governor of Massachusetts.

John Quincy Adams (1767–1848), the oldest son of John Adams, was a diplomat and the U.S. secretary of state from 1817 to 1825. In 1824, he was elected the sixth U.S. president, and he served one term (1825–29). Like his father, he was generally unpopular, because he could not bear to court political favor. Remarkably, he re-entered politics after leaving the presidency by winning election to the U.S. House of Representatives. There he reigned as "Old Man Eloquent," speaking out against slavery and the Mexican War.

John's son Charles Francis Adams (1807–86) served as ambassador to Great Britain during the **Civil War**. He labored successfully to keep Britain neutral during the conflict between the North and the South.

Astor
Financiers and politicians

John Jacob Astor 1864-1912

The Astor family's rise to wealth and power began with **John Jacob Astor** (1763–1848). The son of a butcher, he left his hometown of Waldorf, Germany, at the age of 16 and emigrated first to London, then eventually to New York.

During the 1780s, Astor learned about the fur trade while taking a trip up the Hudson River. He soon decided to make it his career, and by the mid-1790s, he was a leading fur merchant. Astor established the **American Fur Company** in 1808 to compete against the Hudson's Bay Company; Astor's company thrived and soon became the first U.S. monopoly.

After 1834, Astor concentrated on buying property. He built **Astor House**, the first of many family hotels, in New York City. At the time of his death in 1848, he left an estate of more than $20 million, the largest fortune in North America at the time.

His son, **William Blackhouse Astor** (1792–1875), expanded his father's real estate holdings, and earned the nickname of "Landlord of New York." His disregard for the living conditions of his tenants brought him much criticism. He attempted to save his reputation by renovating some of the Astors' older tenements and adding to the Astor Library, which later became a part of the New York Public Library.

William Waldorf Astor (1848–1919), great grandson of John Jacob, focused his ambitions on politics and held several positions in the U.S. government. Unsatisfied with opportunities in America, he moved to London in 1890 and began a career as a newspaper publisher. He became a British subject in 1899, Baron Astor of Hever Castle in 1916, and then 1st Viscount of Hever Castle in 1917.

His son, also named William Waldorf Astor (1879–1952), served as a member of Parliament representing Plymouth, England, from 1910 to 1919. When he succeeded his father as 2nd Viscount of Hever Castle, he gained a seat in the House of Lords. His wife, **Nancy Astor**, ran for and won his seat in the House of Commons. She became the first woman to serve in the British Parliament, and represented Plymouth from 1919 until 1945.

At the same time, the American branch of the family continued to prosper. **John Jacob Astor** (1864–1912), great-grandson of the first John Jacob, built several major New York hotels: the Astoria, the Knickerbocker, and the St. Regis. He was a passenger on board the *HMS Titanic* when it sunk in 1912, and he died in the tragedy. His son, Vincent Astor (1891–1959), became a magazine publisher and also actively managed the family's real estate.

The Augustus family—which descended from **Julius Caesar**—governed the early Roman Empire as emperors for more than four generations.

The first of these descendants was Gaius Octavius (63 B.C.–A.D. 14)—later called **Octavian**—who was Caesar's grandnephew and adopted heir. After Caesar's death, Octavian fought with Mark Antony and **Cleopatra** for control of the Roman Empire. Octavian won the critical Battle of Actium in 31 B.C. and became the first emperor of the Roman Empire. In 27 B.C., the Roman Senate awarded him the title *Augustus*, meaning "highly respected." Augustus ruled the Empire for the next 41 years, rebuilding and improving much of Rome, reforming the governments of the Roman provinces, and treating the people honorably.

Having no direct male heir of his own, Augustus chose his stepson **Tiberius** to succeed him as emperor.

Tiberius (42 B.C.–A.D.37) was defensive and suspicious by nature; he was embittered by the long time he had waited for the throne, and ruled with violent displays against the Roman people. Although Tiberius ruled the empire competently, he was extremely unpopular. He named his nephew's son Gaius Caesar, nicknamed **Caligula**, to be his heir and successor.

Although the Romans cheered the death of Tiberius, they were soon dismayed by Caligula (A.D. 12–41). Already somewhat unbalanced when he assumed power at a young age, Caligula quickly went mad. Before he was assassinated by one of the *Praetorian* (imperial) bodyguards, Caligula squandered much of the wealth that Tiberius had amassed.

In the chaos that followed Caligula's murder, the Praetorian Guards found Claudius (10 B.C.–A.D.54), Caligula's uncle, hiding behind a curtain and named him emperor. Deeply knowledgeable, he administered the empire wisely and expanded it to include Britain. Claudius's downfall was his choice in wives. His first wife, Messalina, was power-mad, and Claudius agreed to her execution; his second wife, **Agrippina**, poisoned him when she learned he did not favor her son Nero, from an earlier marriage.

Claudius and Agrippina

Nero (A.D. 37–68) was a great grandnephew of Augustus. He was adopted by Claudius in A.D. 50; upon Claudius' death, Nero's mother Agrippina secured the throne for him at the age of 16. Nero administered well for five years; but then he began to exhibit the madness and cruelty of some of his ancestors.

He murdered both his mother and his first wife. When a great fire devastated Rome in A.D. 64, he took advantage of the city's destruction to build new monuments to himself. In A.D. 68, a revolt broke out against him in the province of **Gaul** (modern-day France) and Nero fled. He committed suicide later that year—the last male descendant of the Caesar-Augustus line.

Bach
German musicians

Johann Sebastian Bach

The Bach name shines brightly in the field of classical music. Possibly no other family has invented as many music styles nor set the standard for as long as the Bachs of Germany.

Johann Sebastian Bach (1685–1750) was born in Eisenach, Thuringia (modern-day **Germany**), into a family of musicians—his father and brother probably gave him his first music lessons. Although orphaned at 10, Bach continued to study and developed skill as a performer and composer of keyboard and church music. At 18, he took the job of church organist in Arnstadt, and four years later, in Mülhausen. He married his second cousin, **Maria Barbara Bach**, in 1707 and they had seven children.

Following the death of his wife in 1720, Bach married **Anna Magdalena Wilcken** in 1721; Bach then began a second family that numbered 13 children.

In 1723 Bach became music director for the city of **Leipzig** and cantor of the St. Thomas School. In Leipzig, Bach quarreled bitterly and frequently with his employers, who did not meet his demands for good musicians, decent facilities, or an adequate salary.

More famous as a performer than a composer during his lifetime, Bach nevertheless composed groundbreaking works for keyboard and orchestra in the fugue form, the core of the Baroque style of music. The fugues in his famous *Brandenburg Concertos* demonstrate this counterpoint of several melodies over and under a main melody. Bach wrote *The Well-Tempered Clavier* as a series of lessons in the fugue and in an equal use of both hands on the keyboard—a first in musical history.

Wilhelm Friedemann Bach (1710–84) was the oldest child of Bach's first marriage. Born in Weimar, he showed great musical talent at an early age. Unfortunately, he also displayed a difficult personality. Wilhelm was the organist and music director for a church in Halle between 1746 and 1764, but then was employed only irregularly for the remaining 20 years of his life.

Carl Philipp Emmanuel Bach (1714–88) was also born in Weimar. He entered the service of King Frederick the Great of Prussia in 1740, and became the director of chamber music of the Prussian court. After retiring from court service in 1767, he served as the musical director for various churches in Hamburg from 1767 to 1788.

Johann Christian Bach (1735–82) was the youngest of Johann Sebastian's 20 children. Born in Leipzig, he became a composer for the King's Theater in London in 1762—earning the nickname of the "English Bach." He was a master of orchestration and a composer of fine melodies.

6. Barca
Carthaginian military leaders

To keep their country from being overtaken by the Roman Empire, the Barca family of Carthage in northern Africa fought long and courageoulsy.

Hamilcar Barca (c. 270–229 B.C.) was a Carthaginian general who fought against the Roman Empire during the **First Punic War** (264-241 B.C.) He led his troops in northern Sicily against the Romans, but was deafeated by them. **Carthage** surrendered Siciliy to Rome, and Hamiclar returned to Africa. Hamilcar left Carthage in 237 B.C. for Spain, and brought his family with him—including Hannibal (247–183 B.C.), his nine-year-old son.

The Barcas created a new Carthaginian colony in Spain. Hamilcar drowned while his troops were withdrawing from a siege of the town of Helice. Leadership of the family passed to **Hasdrubal**, a son-in-law of Hamilcar. Hasdrubal founded Cartagena (New Carthage) on the southwestern coast of Spain. Spanish chieftains assassinated Hasdrubal in 221 B.C.

Hamilcar's son **Hannibal** became supreme commander in Spain and leader of the family. Already a hardened warrior, he ached for an opportunity to strike at Rome, which had humbled his native city in the First Punic War. Hannibal laid siege to the Spanish city of Sanguntum, an ally of Rome. When he refused to abandon the siege, Rome declared war on Carthage, beginning the **Second Punic War** in 218 B.C.

Hannibal left his younger brother, also named Hasdrubal, in command in Spain. Hannibal led more than 35,000 Carthaginian, Spanish, and Gaulish troops as well as a number of elephants over the Pyrenees and Alps to invade northern Italy. His greatest victory came at the Battle of Cannae (216 B.C.). In one day, he destroyed two Roman armies and 50,000 Romans lost their lives.

Hannibal's military genius was not enough to overcome the strength and resilience of the Roman empire. The Italian city-states remained loyal to Rome and Hannibal was essentially marooned in Italy, unable to strike a final blow.

Seeking to rendezvous with his older brother, Hasdrubal marched his force of 10,000 men into a trap at the Battle of the Metaurus River and they were destroyed. Hannibal only learned of his brother's fate when a Roman horseman threw Hasdrubal's head into his camp.

Hannibal returned to Africa and fought the Battle of Zama (202 B.C.) against **Scipio II**. After his defeat, Hannibal urged his city to seek peace with Rome. Hannibal left Carthage a few years later, and stirred up trouble for the Romans in the eastern Mediterranean by encouraging the king of **Syria** to go to war against the empire. After the Romans defeated Syria, they pursued Hannibal relentlessly. Rather than surrender to his eternal foes, Hannibal committed suicide by taking poison.

Hannibal crossing the Alps

Barrymore
American actors

Georgiana Drew Barrymore and children

Known as the "Royal Family of Broadway," the **Barrymores** are perhaps the most famous family of American actors, with members from four generations performing on stage and screen.

The family was founded by **Herbert Blythe** (1847–1905), who later adopted the stage name Maurice Barrymore. Born in Fort Agra, India, Blythe immigrated to the United States in 1875. He married actress **Georgiana Emma Drew** (1856–93) the following year, and the couple toured and performed together in 1878 and 1879 before settling down in Philadelphia.

Lionel Barrymore (1878–1954), the eldest of Maurice and Georgiana's three children, made his first stage appearance in 1893. The advent of "talkies," motion pictures with sound, was a great boon to his career. Lionel starred in *A Free Soul* (1931), winning an Academy Award for best actor. He later became a well-known character actor, starring in such films as *Captains Courageous* (1937), *Duel in the Sun* (1947), and *It's a Wonderful Life* (1948).

Ethel Barrymore (1879–1959), Lionel's sister, made her stage debut in New York City in

1894 in a company headed by her grandmother, Louisa Drew. Ethel first starred on Broadway in 1901, and she played a succession of important Shakespearean roles from 1922 to 1926. In 1933 she appeared in *Rasputin and the Empress,* the only film she made with her brothers Lionel and John. She won an Academy Award for her performance in the 1944 film, *None but the Lonely Heart.*

Younger brother **John Barrymore** (1882–1942) made his theatrical debut in 1903. By 1922, he was acclaimed as the greatest Shakespearean actor of his day. Nicknamed the "Great Profile," he soon turned to motion pictures, giving notable performances in *Don Juan* (1926), *Twentieth Century* (1932), and *Romeo and Juliet* (1936).

Diana Barrymore (1921–60) was the daughter of John and his second wife, poetess Michael Strange. Diana made her Broadway debut in 1939, and achieved great success with her role in the film Ladies Courageous (1945). Her autobiography, *Too Much, Too Soon* (1957) was one of the first of its kind to point to the connection between early stardom and alcoholism.

John Barrymore, Jr. (b. 1932) was the son of John and his third wife, actress Dolores Costello. Using the stage name of John Drew Barrymore, he made his film debut in *The Sundowners* (1950).

His daughter, **Drew Barrymore** (b. 1975), made her first acting appearance at the age of three in the television movie, *Suddenly Love.* Drew is probably best known as the little girl who befriends an alien in Steven Spielberg's *E.T.: The Extra-Terrestrial* (1982).

The Bellini family of Venice produced three great Renaissance painters. **Jacopo Bellini** (c. 1400–c. 1470) was born in **Venice**, but little is known of his early years. He studied painting with Gentile de Fabriano, one of the most influential painters in Italy at the time. Bellini accompanied his artistic master to Florence in 1423 and returned to Venice in 1429.

Bellini emphasized the use of gold pigment in works such as his *Madonna* (c. 1438). Following other painters of his day, Bellini painted religious themes almost exclusively in his early works. For a long time, he retained **Byzantine** influences in his art, and then later began to emphasize the renaissance style of perspective, landscape, and classical beauty.

Perhaps even more important than his paintings were the two notebooks of drawings that Bellini made around 1450. In the drawings, he experimented with the use of linear perspective. He was among the first artists to make figures diminish as they receded into space. His work influenced an entire generation of artists who followed him, his sons Gentile and Giovanni among them.

Gentile Bellini (c. 1429–1507) was most likely trained to paint by his father. He is best known for his huge canvas paintings of the people and buildings of Venice. He paid great attention to detail, giving even the smallest of his figures recognizable features. The Doge (duke), the hereditary ruler of Venice, sent Gentile to Constantinople in 1479 to paint for the sultan of the **Ottoman Empire**. Gentile's single best-known work is *Portrait of Mohammad II*, painted around 1480.

The most famous of the Bellini artists was Jacopo's son Giovanni Bellini (c. 1430–1516), who also trained with his father. His long artistic career showed a slow evolution from the painting of religious narratives to depictions of landscapes and natural light. In his first 20 years of painting, Giovanni concentrated on Madonnas, Pietàs (a representation of the Virgin Mary mourning over the body of the dead Christ, usually shown held on her lap), and crucifixions. Later he turned to the painting of great historical scenes as the official court painter for the **Venetian Republic**.

In addition to his official paintings for the court, Giovanni maintained his own studio and a large workshop of students, including such famous painters as **Titian** (1487-1576) and Giorgione (1476-1510). Students from across Europe came to apprentice with **Giovanni**, and returned home greatly influenced by his style. In his later works, he created such accurate outdoor scenes and effects of light that a viewer could determine not only the season depicted in the painting, but also the approximate hour of the day.

Doge of Venice **by Giovanni Bellini**

Bernoulli
Swiss scientists and mathematicians

When students use calculus or figure statistical probabilities, they often use formulas that were created by members of one special family of scientists and mathematicians: the Bernoullis of Basel, Switzerland.

Jakob Bernoulli (1654–1705), started the family on the road to scientific careers. He departed from the family pharmacology business and studied mathematics and astronomy at the University of Basel. He became a professor there in 1687. Jakob developed the **Law of Large Numbers**, which stated that any assigned degree of probability can be determined by increasing the number of trials (such as in throwing dice).

Jakob's younger brother Johann (1667–1748) was the 10th child in the family. He studied medicine and mathematics, and became a professor of mathematics at the University of Groningen in the Netherlands. The two brothers often worked

Johann Bernoulli

on the same problems, sometimes quarreling about the solutions. When Jakob died, Johann replaced him at the University of Basel.

Nikolaus Bernoulli (1687–1759)—whose father had been an alderman and a painter—was a nephew of Jakob and Johann. Nikolaus studied both mathematics and law. He then taught mathematics at the University of Padua in Italy and logic and the law at the University of Basel.

Daniel (1700–82) was one of Johann's sons. He studied medicine and mathematics, and went to St. Petersburg to teach mathematics at the **Academy of Sciences**. He returned to Switzerland in 1732 , and taught anatomy, botany, physiology, and physics. Daniel solved a differential equation that has become known as **Bernoulli's Principle**. The principle states that when the movement of fluid speeds up, fluid pressure lessens. This principle had significant applications for the design of aircraft, boats, and fluid conduit systems.

Johann II (1710–90) was the youngest child of Johann. A resident of Switzerland for his entire life, he conducted research on the theory of heat and light and received the prize of the French Academy three times. His son Johann III (1744–1807) was a recognized child prodigy. He earned his doctorate in law at the age of 14 and went to Prussia where King **Frederick the Great** (see no. 50) commissioned him to organize the Academy of Berlin's astronomical center.

Jakob II (1759–89) was the younger son of Johann II. He succeeded his uncle, Daniel, as professor of mathematics at the University of St. Petersburg. He suffered a tragic, early death from drowning, while swimming in the Neva River.

For a brief time at the beginning of the 19th century, members of the Bonaparte family ruled over much of Europe.

Napoleon Bonaparte (1769–1821)—the family's most famous member—came from **Corsica**, a Mediterranean island under French rule with an Italian history. His father, Carlo Buonaparte (1746–85), was a member of the lower Corsican nobility.

Napoleon studied at French military academies, and soon after the **French Revolution** began in 1789, he threw in his lot with the revolutionaries. He rose rapidly through the ranks during the 1790s, primarily due to his military victories in northern Italy. In 1799, he returned to France, and overthrew the ruling **Directory**. He established a Consulate government, and named himself **First Consul**. By 1804 he had become emperor and absolute ruler of France.

During the decade of his greatest military successes—1800-1810—Napoleon was able to place many of his relatives on the thrones of smaller European nations. His brother Joseph (1768–1844) became King of Naples, then King of all of Spain, where he ruled from 1808 until 1813. Brother Louis (1778–1846) was made King of Holland at the same time. The youngest of the children, brother Jérôme (1784–1860), became king of Westphalia in Prussia in 1807.

Napoleon's sisters fared well because of their brother's power. Pauline (1780–1825) became duchess of **Guastalla** in northern Italy in 1806. Caroline (1782–1839), the sibling most like Napoleon in ambition, became queen of Naples in 1808. Élisa (1777–1820) became grand duchess of **Tuscany** in 1809.

By 1810 the Bonapartes (the French version of Buonaparte) occupied the thrones of a majority of the countries of Europe. However, the end of their reigns came swiftly.

Napoleon

Napoleon was defeated in his war against **Russia** in 1812. He abdicated the throne of France in 1814 and all of his siblings lost their positions and titles. Napoleon's brief comeback during the **Hundred Days' War** of 1815 did not bring a return to the former glory. The **Duke of Wellington** handed the former emperor his most resounding defeat at **Waterloo** on June 18, 1805. He died in exile on the tiny island of St. Helena.

In the mid 19th century, a member of the next generation of Bonapartes came to power. Louis-Napoleon (1808–73), son of Louis, was elected president of the Second French Republic in 1848. The young president staged a coup d'etat in 1851 and proclaimed himself **Emperor Napoleon III**. He ruled France until its defeat in the Franco-Prussian War of 1870; Napoleon III then abdicated and lived in exile in England.

A family of actors named Booth made their mark on the stage—and in the history books—of 19th-century America.

The family's founder, **Junius Brutus Booth** (1796–1852), was born in London, England. He made his stage debut in 1817, playing Iago in Shakespeare's *Othello*, with famous British actor Edmund Kean in the title role. Following Booth's success in England, he decided to expand his horizons and seek fame in America.

Edwin and daughter Edwina Booth

Booth and his wife arrived in the United States in 1821. Booth made his American stage debut in **Richmond**, Virginia, playing King Richard III. This soon became his stock role, and he went on to perform it around the country.

Their son **Edwin Booth** (1833–93) grew up playing Tressel to his father's Richard III.

In 1851 Edwin played Richard III himself for the first time and was an instant hit. His father's death the following year opened new opportunities for him to shine in his own right. In 1863 he leased the **Winter Garden Theater** in New York City. The next year, he played Hamlet for 100 consecutive performances, the greatest run of a single actor in America up to that time. In April 1865, his career was temporarily threatened by the actions of his younger brother, John.

Born on the family farm, **John Wilkes Booth** (1838–65) was an athletic and handsome boy. He played on the stage with considerable success, although he was never a dedicated actor; his natural talent carried him through many poorly rehearsed roles. Unlike the rest of the Booth family, John was vehemently in favor of the Confederate cause during the Civil War. He devised a plot to kidnap President **Abraham Lincoln** in 1864. When that scheme failed, he joined with others to plan the murder of the president.

On the evening of April 14, 1865, Booth entered Ford's Theater in Washington, D.C., and shot Lincoln in the back of the head, killing him. Booth then leaped from the presidential box to the floor of the stage and shouted, *"Sic semper tyrannis!"* ("Thus ever to tyrants!") He escaped from Washington, but was soon caught and killed by soldiers while in hiding on a farm near Bowling Green, Virginia.

Ashamed of his brother's action, Edwin retired temporarily from the stage. He returned in January 1866 and played Hamlet again. He built his own theater in New York in 1868, but went bankrupt in 1874. Booth retired from the stage in 1891. Despite the tragedy of his brother's actions, he was known as the "Prince of Players," and generally recognized as the foremost American actor of the 19th century.

Borgia
Italian religious and military leaders

Cesare Borgia

The Borgias were an ambitious family of religious and military leaders who personified the glory and terror of the Italian Renaissance.

Rodrigo Borgia (1431–1503) was born in Xativa, Spain, near Valencia. He became a ward of his maternal uncle, Cardinal Alfonso de Borgia. In 1455, when Alfonso became Pope **Callistus III**, Rodrigo followed his uncle to Rome and was made a cardinal of the **Catholic Church** the following year.

Charismatic as well as thoroughly unscrupulous, Rodrigo made a fortune during the papacy of his uncle. He bought and sold pardons, indulgences (the forgiveness of sins), and church offices. He fathered a number of illegitimate children, of whom his favorites—Cesare and Lucrezia—were born to his mistress, Vannozza Catanei.

Rodrigo successfully bribed the College of Cardinals and was elected **Pope Alexander VI** in August 1492. As pope, Alexander openly acknowledged his children. He spent a great deal of papal revenue on attempts to forward the career of his son, Cesare.

Cesare Borgia (c. 1475–1507) became a cardinal in 1493. He alternated between important diplomatic missions for the **Vatican** and a salacious life in Rome. He renounced his religious duties in 1498. Sent by his father to France to bestow papal blessings on the marriage of King **Louis XII** to Ann of Brittany, Cesare himself found a bride on the mission—Charlotte d'Albret, sister of the king of Navarre.

Cesare returned to Italy and sought to gain military control over the central part of the peninsula. He made two victorious campaigns, and by 1503 he controlled Romagna, Umbria, and the Marches.

In 1503 Alexander VI died after contracting a serious fever. To his astonishment, Cesare was attacked by foes from all directions once his powerful father was gone. He was arrested and made to surrender the forts he had acquired. When Julius II was elected to the papal throne, Cesare fled and eventually made his way to Navarre where he died fighting as a soldier for that principality.

Pope Alexander VI's daughter **Lucrezia Borgia** (1480–1519) was born in Subiaco, Italy. By the time she was 22, her father and brother had arranged successive marriages for her to Italian princes Giovanni Sforza, Alfonso of Aragon, and Alfonso d'Este for their own political gains. Renowned as a scheming poisoner, after her father's death in 1503, she led an exemplary life. Her last husband became the Duke of Ferrara, and as a true child of Italian courtly society, she encouraged the work of writers, artists, and painters, and helped make Ferrara a center of Renaissance art.

13. Bourbon
European monarchs

The **Bourbon** family of French, Spanish, and Italian monarchs was originally a branch of the Capet family, which ruled France from A.D. 987 until 1337 (see no. 21). The first duke of Bourbon, Louis, was the sixth son of King **Louis IX** (1214–70) of France. The king passed the duchy on to his son and the Bourbons produced male heirs for the next six generations.

By the early 1500s, the title of duke went to **Charles de Bourbon** who also acquired the duchy of Vendôme. Charles's grandson became King of Navarre, and then became the first Bourbon to sit on the throne of France as King Henry IV (reigned 1589–1610). When he was assassinated in 1610, the throne went to his son **Louis XIII** (reigned 1610–43); he was succeeded by his son, the "boy king" Louis XIV (reigned 1643–1715).

Louis XVI leaving his family

Louis XIV had the palace of Versailles built to commemorate the glory of France and the Bourbon family. Seeking to augment the strength of the family, he placed his grandson, Philip d'Anjou, on the throne of Spain. Philip became King **Philip V** (reigned 1700–46), the first in the line of Spanish Bourbon monarchs.

The French Bourbon monarchs continued with **Louis XV** (reigned 1715–74) as king, followed by Louis XVI (reigned 1774–92), who was overthrown and beheaded in 1793 during the French Revolution. His two younger brothers later returned to France as King Louis XVIII (reigned 1814–24) and King Charles X (reigned 1824–30). The Bourbon dynasty ended in France with the French Revolution of 1830, which ousted Charles X.

The **Spanish Bourbons** brought a renaissance of culture to Spain during the 18th century. Even the turbulence of the French Revolution and Napoleonic wars failed to topple them. Napoleon installed his brother Joseph as King of Spain for five years (1808-1813). However, after Napoleon's defeat, the Bourbon line returned to the throne with **Ferdinand VII** (reigned 1814–33). The family line continued through Isabella II (reigned 1833–68), Alfonso XII (reigned 1874–85), and Alfonso XIII (reigned 1886–1931).

Two other branches of the Bourbon family ruled in Italy. Philip Bourbon became the duke of Parma (reigned 1720–65), and the line continued until Robert, Duke of Parma, was ousted in the Italian nationalist revolution in 1859. Ferdinand IV became King of Naples in 1799—his reign until 1820 was repeatedly usurped by Napoleon. Francis II, King of the Two Sicilies until 1860, was overthrown by the followers of Guiseppe Garibaldi.

14. Braganza
Portuguese and Brazilian rulers

The **Braganza** family of Portuguese and Brazilian rulers came from the town of the same name in northeastern **Portugal**.

Alfonso of Braganza was made the first Duke of Braganza in 1422. Following his death in 1461, the family remained members of the lower nobility until Joao I—the sixth duke of Braganza—married the niece of King John III of Portugal. This established the Braganza family's claim to membership within the royal family line.

Portugal was invaded and conquered by the Spanish forces of King **Philip II** in 1580 (see no. 46). In December, 1640, Joao II, the eighth duke of Braganza, headed the rebellion that overthrew Spanish rule. Joao II took the new title of King **John IV** of Portugal (reigned 1640–56), and from then on, the heir to the Portuguese throne was known as the Duke of Braganza.

Throughout the reigns of Alfonso VI (1656-1667), Peter II (1667-1706), John V (1706-1750), Portugal's standing in Europe underwent very little change. By the 18th century, the days of Portuguese wealth from the overseas trade of silk and spices ended, and Portugal then depended on Great Britain economically. However, during the reign of **Joseph I** (1750-1777), the government was controlled by the powerful Sebastião José de Carvalho—the Marquis de Pombal. Ruthless and heartless, Pombal broke the power of the privileged nobility and the Church.

Marquis de Pombal

Joseph's daughter—Maria I (1734–1816)—and her husband Pedro III (1717–1786) jointly took the throne in 1777. After Peter's death, Mary continued to rule, but much of the power went to her son, who would become King **John VI** (1816–1826).

When soldiers of Napoleonic France invaded Portugal in 1807, John VI was forced into exile. He fled to Rio de Janeiro and declared that Brazil—formerly a colony—and Portugal would be one kingdom. After Napoleon's defeat in 1815, John VI ruled Portugal from Brazil until 1821 when he returned to Lisbon, leaving his son Pedro to rule in Brazil.

Portugal and Brazil became separate nations in 1822. John VI ruled in Lisbon and Pedro became Emperor **Pedro I** (reigned 1822–31) of Brazil. Following John's death, Pedro crossed the Atlantic and became King Pedro IV (reigned 1826) of Portugal. He abdicated both thrones to his children; his daughter became Queen **Maria II** (reigned 1826–1853) of Portugal while his son became Emperor Pedro II (reigned 1831–1889) of Brazil. In 1889 Pedro II was deposed when Brazil became a republic.

The Portuguese dynasty staggered on through the 19th century. The final monarch—King Manuel II (reigned 1908–1910) —was deposed by the Portuguese military in October, 1910 when Portugal became a republic.

The millions of people who have read *Wuthering Heights* and other novels written by the **Brontë** sisters can identify much of the fictional pain and suffering as the Brontë family's own.

The founder and father of the family—**Patrick Brontë**—was born in Ireland in 1777. In 1812, he married Maria Branwell, and the couple settled in Haworth in **Yorkshire**, England, where they raised six children: Maria, Elizabeth, Charlotte, Patrick Branwell, Emily Jane, and Anne.

Maria and Elizabeth Brontë both died while attending the Clergy Daughters' School in Lancashire. The four younger siblings also inherited their parents' delicate constitutions. Better protected by living at Haworth, they read and wrote together constantly.

In 1842, Charlotte (1816–1855) and Emily (1818–1848) went to Brussels, **Belgium**, to study languages; they planned to open a school of their own and would need to be certified to teach foreign language. By 1845 they had returned to Haworth, and the four siblings again dedicated all their energies to literary pursuits. Because of the discrimina-tion faced by women writers at the time, the three sisters wrote their first books under the male pseudonym Bell. As "Ellis Bell," Emily wrote *Wuthering Heights*, published in 1847. Anne (1820–1849) wrote *Agnes Grey* under the name "Acton Bell" and Charlotte wrote *The Professor* under the name of "Currer Bell."

All three sisters began to use their true names after 1847. Charlotte's novel *Jane Eyre* was published that year. Anne published *The Tenant of Wildfell Hall* in 1848, the same year that Patrick Bronwell died. Tragedy continued to strike the family: Emily died of tuberculo-sis later in the same year, and Anne died early in 1849.

Stricken and desolate, Charlotte lived alone at **Haworth** with her father. She published *Villette* in 1853 and married the Reverend **Arthur Nicholls**, curate of Haworth, in 1854. Charlotte died of pregnancy toxemia one year after her marriage. Her widowed husband remained in Haworth until his father-in-law died and then went to Ireland, completing a family circle that had begun with Patrick Brontë's emigration to England.

The Brontës

The Brontës endured sor-row and desolation, yet they pro-duced a remarkable and diverse body of literature. The Brontë sisters wrote books that spoke to the romantic sensibilities and cul-tural limitations of their era. Men were heroic but flawed; women endured all the pain and suffering as part of their duty in life. The settings of the Brontë stories—English moors and run-down family estates—contributed to the development of the **Gothic** romance novel, a genre that con-tinued to evolve for generations.

16. Bruce
Scottish rulers

Identified with the freedom of Scotland, the **Bruce** family of popular leaders originally came from Normandy. The name "Bruce" was derived from *Bruis*, a castle near Cherbourg in the French province of Normandy. Robert de Bruce crossed the English Channel in the Norman invasion of 1066 and received lands from William the Conqueror as a reward for his help.

Robert II (c. 1078–1141) held the lands his father had been given; he also received a *fief* (estate) in southern Scotland called **Annandale**. The land holdings of the Bruce family straddled the border of England and Scotland for the next two centuries.

The Bruce claim to the throne of **Scotland** had its origin in the marriage of Robert IV (c.1150- 1191) to Isabella, one of the daughters of King William the Lion of Scotland.

Robert VI "the Competitor" (1210–1295) was one of the 13 claimants to the throne, after King Alexander died in 1290. He and his son, Robert VII (1253–1304), both agreed to the compromise decision that gave the throne of Scotland to King **Edward I** of England.

This agreement led to fighting on the border between the two countries. **William Wallace**, a commoner, led a rebellion against King Edward. His forces won the Battle of Stirling but were crushed at Falkirk, where Robert VIII —Robert the Bruce— (1274–1329) fought on the side of the English.

Robert the Bruce was torn between his love for Scotland and his loyalty to King Edward, as well as his desire to maintain his estates in England. After witnessing the final defeat and capture of Wallace in 1305, he pledged his allegiance to Scotland, and in 1306, was crowned Robert I, King of Scotland.

Robert's efforts to keep England out were defeated, and King Edward temporarily exiled

Robert the Bruce

him. After the king's death, Robert began the final war for Scottish freedom. He won the crucial **Battle of Bannockburn** in 1314, and a treaty of independence for Scotland by the time of his death in 1329.

Freedom from English rule was by no means assured. Robert's son, David II (reigned 1329–1370), had to continually fight for his right to the throne against English aggressors. He was defeated by an English army in 1333 and went to France. King David was restored to the throne twice, first in 1346 and again in 1357. He died childless. The Scottish throne then passed to the son of his sister Margaret—the daughter of Robert I—who had married Walter "the Steward." Their son Robert II (reigned 1371-1390) established the Stuart line of succession that would rule Scotland for the next 300 years. (see no. 89)

23

The dukes of Burgundy briefly ruled over what could have become the "Middle Kingdom" of western Europe between France and the Holy Roman Empire. The family's origins dates back to 1031, when Robert, the second son of King Robert II of France, was granted the title of **Duke of Burgundy**.

The family ruled over an agriculturally wealthy section of eastern France, centered around **Dijon** (de-zhôn'). In 1361 the last male heir of the family died and the title was passed to Philip, the fourth son of King **John II** of France. Soon known as "Philip the Bold," he ruled over Burgundy between 1364 and 1404. During these years, when England was at war with France, Philip steered a middle course, and at times, even favored the English. This course, which some called traitorous, led both France and England to court Burgundy's favor during the **Hundred Years' War**.

Duke John the Fearless (reigned 1404–1419) was killed by followers of the Valois kings during a meeting held under a flag of truce. From that time, the leaders of Burgundy vowed vengeance on France.

Duke **Philip the Good** (reigned 1419–1467) presided over a period of Burgundian wealth and power. His dukedom rivaled both France and England in military strength, and he showed a clear desire to create Burgundy as a separate kingdom.

Due to favorable marriages, Philip the Good acquired a much greater amount of territory than had his predecessors. While he ruled over the dukedom of Burgundy, Philip was also liege lord—the feudal lord entitled to allegiance and service—in the territories of Flanders, Brabant, Hainut, Luxembourg, Limburg, Gelderland, Zeeland, Holland, Artois, and part of Picardy.

During Philip's reign, Dijon became an artistic center; painters traveled across the region to settle in the rich, fertile valleys of Burgundy. Bruges and Brussels also thrived as centers for painting and music. This was truly the height of the **"Burgundian Renaissance."** Much of the present knowledge of medieval life comes from tapestries woven during the lifetime of Philip the Good.

Charles the Bold

Duke **Charles the Bold** (reigned 1467–77) faced a more formidable France, one that was victorious in the Hundred Years' War. France's King Louis XI—the "Spider King"—created an alliance with the Holy Roman Empire and preyed on Burgundian territory. The demise of Burgundy as a power came about largely because of the impatience of Charles, who threw his men into combat against Swiss troops at the Battle of Nancy in 1477. The duchy of Burgundy disappeared after his death.

18. Bush
American politicians

The Bush family has provided America with three generations of political leaders during the 20th century.

Prescott Sheldon Bush (1902–63), a Republican from Connecticut, served in the U.S. Senate from 1953 to 1963. He married Dorothy Walker and they had one son, **George Herbert Walker Bush** (b. 1924). As a young man, George attended Phillips Academy, and after World War II began, he entered the U.S. Navy in 1942. He flew 58 combat missions, and on one mission was shot down over the Pacific.

The Bush Family

Bush married **Barbara Pierce** in 1945. The couple had four sons and two daughters, the youngest of whom, Robin, died at an early age.

Bush earned his B.A. from Yale University in 1948. He then went to Texas and entered the oil business. However, even as he accumulated wealth from oil, his greatest ambition was to succeed in politics.

Bush won election to the U.S. House of Representatives in 1967, but failed in a bid to win a seat in the U.S. Senate in 1970. His loyalty to the **Republican Party** earned him several jobs during the 1970s under Republican presidents: ambassador to the United Nations (1971-1973); ambassador to Communist China (1974 -1975); and director of the Central Intelligence Agency (1975-1977).

Bush ran for the Republican presidential nomination in 1980, but lost the nomination to former California governor Ronald Reagan. Bush then accepted the nomination as Reagan's vice presidential running mate, and served as vice president during Reagan's two terms, from 1981 to 1989.

Bush ran for and won the Republican presidential nomination in 1988. He then defeated Democratic governor **Michael Dukakis** of Massachusetts in the general election.

As president, Bush excelled in the intricacies of foreign policy. However, Bush was vulnerable to criticisms of his domestic policy. The American economy slumped badly between 1990 and 1992. In a presidential campaign that saw additional competition from third-party candidate, Texas billionaire Ross Perot, Bush lost the 1992 election to the savvy Democratic governor of Arkansas, **Bill Clinton**. Bush then retired to private life.

His son **George Walker Bush** (b. 1946) ran for and won election as governor of Texas in 1994. In 1998, he was re-elected as Texas's governor, while his younger brother Jeb Bush (b. 1953) won the governorship in Florida.

As the campaign for the 2000 national election got underway, George Walker Bush was considered the leading candidate to capture the Republican presidential nomination.

William Byrd II

Among the members of the American Byrd family can be found several generations of distinguished politicians, and a daring explorer of the Antarctic continent.

The family's political roots began with **William Byrd** (1652–1705). Born in London, he moved to the **Virginia** colony when he was 18, to settle 1,800 acres of land he inherited at the Falls of the James River (present-day Richmond). He held high offices in the colony, serving in the **House of Burgesses** from 1677 to 1682. Byrd had one son and three daughters with his wife, Mary Horsmanden.

One son, **William Byrd II** (1674–1744), was born in Virginia but educated in London. He returned to Virginia in 1696 and served briefly in the House of Burgesses. William II greatly increased the family land holdings; by the time of his death, he owned 180,000 acres and a 4,000-volume library, the largest in all the colonies. During the 20th century, his letters and diaries were discovered and edited, giving scholars and historians remarkable insight into the life of a great country gentleman in colonial America.

The brothers Harry Flood Byrd (1887–1966) and **Richard Evelyn Byrd** (1888–1957) were direct descendants of William Byrd II. Their father was a prominent newspaper publisher.

Harry Byrd entered politics. He served in the Virginia senate from 1915 to 1925 and then as governor of the state from 1926 to 1930. Having established a political machine that would dominate Virginia politics for more than a generation, Harry went on to serve in the U.S. Senate from 1933 to 1965. Byrd vigilantly studied **New Deal** legislation of the Great Depression to determine its impact on the American national debt. He resigned his Senate seat in 1965 so his son Harry Flood Byrd, Jr., could be appointed to take his place. Harry Jr. won the seat by election in 1966 and served there until 1983.

Richard Byrd was one of the most intrepid of American explorers. Born in Winchester, Virginia, he served in the U.S. Navy and then trained as an aviator. He commanded U.S. Air Forces of Canada in 1918.

With **Floyd Bennett** as his copilot, Richard made the first flight over the North Pole on May 9, 1926. He also made the first flight over the South Pole on November 28 and 29, 1929. Following this feat, Richard was promoted to rear admiral in the U.S. Navy. By the time he died, Byrd had led a total of five expeditions to Antarctica.

A father and son named Cabot paved the way for European exploration and settlement of the Americas.

John Cabot's real name was **Giovanni Caboto**, and he was born in Genoa, Italy, around 1450. He moved to **Venice** as a young boy and became a full citizen of that city in 1475. He became a trader with merchants in the eastern Mediterranean Sea. In Venice, he heard the remarkable stories about **Marco Polo** (see no. 78), who had traveled overland to China during the 13th century.

Cabot married Mattea, a Venetian woman, around 1480. They had three sons: Ludovico, Sebastian, and Sancio. Cabot moved his family to England in 1495. To all who would listen, he presented his idea of sailing across the Atlantic Ocean by a more northerly route than Columbus had taken to find the "spice islands" of present-day Indonesia.

Cabot received letters of patent from King **Henry VII** of England in 1496, authorizing him to find and hold areas in the Americas for England and promising him a monopoly on any trade he could establish there.

In May 1497, Cabot set sail from Bristol, England, aboard the ship *Matthew*. After a voyage of 35 days, Cabot and his crew landed

Sebastian Cabot

somewhere off the shore of present-day eastern **Canada**. Cabot went ashore, claimed the land for King Henry VII, and made a fast 15-day return crossing from Newfoundland to England. Cabot was convinced he had found part of Asia. He had been astonished by the tremendous schools of fish off Newfoundland, and reported everything to the king.

In May 1498, Cabot set sail again, this time with five ships. One ship returned and reported bad storms; Cabot and the other ships were never heard from again.

After his father's disappearance, **Sebastian Cabot** (c. 1476–1557) vowed to continue the family legacy by exploring the Americas. He set sail on his first major voyage in 1508, and took two ships to Iceland, Greenland, and Labrador in Canada. Cabot then sailed south to the coast of **Virginia** before he returned to England.

Cabot left England and entered the service of Spain in 1512. In 1526 he was given command of a major Spanish expedition to reach the Pacific Ocean by way of South America. Cabot and his fleet only made it as far as the Rio de la Plata between present-day Uruguay and Paraguay. Having won little distinction or glory for Spain, Cabot returned to England. In 1548 he was made a geographical adviser and granted a royal pension.

Capet
French rulers

In A.D. 987 the Frank nobles gathered to elect a new king because the last male heir of the Carolingian dynasty had died. The nobles selected **Hugh Capet** (c. A.D. 938–996), who was descended from Robert the Strong, a ninth-century count in the kingdom of the West Franks.

Capet acquired the title of king, but he did not have the power normally associated with it. He had direct control over only the two counties of Paris and Orléans. During the reign of Capet, and those of his first five successors, the family managed to change the monarchy from an elective into a hereditary one.

Election of Hugh Capet

The Capetians also slowly extended their power beyond the boundaries of the two counties. They were cautious in their movements since they did not want to offend the prominent nobles, some of whom controlled more land than they did. One of the nobles, Duke William of Normandy, became King of England in 1066. Duke William, who owed his allegiance to the Capetian family, now had another entire kingdom to rule. That situation would lead to many conflicts between England, France, and Normandy in the years to come.

The seventh Capetian king, **Philip II Augustus** (reigned 1180–1223), acquired greater power for the family. Although he fought in the **Third Crusade** with King Richard the Lion-Hearted of England in 1187, Philip plotted against England and managed to capture the areas of Normandy, Anjou, and Maine. Philip's conquest of these regions was completed by his victory at the Battle of Bouvines against the **Holy Roman Empire** in 1214. By the time of his death, he had brought most of present-day France under the control of the Capetian dynasty.

King **Louis IX** (reigned 1226–70) was an anomaly in 13th-century Europe. He was a king who was truly a Christian. Beloved by his subjects for his sense of mercy and justice, Louis presided over a France that had become the most powerful nation in Europe. Paris was the center for medieval chivalry and learning, and French customs and culture were the envy of its European neighbors.

Philip IV "the Fair" (reigned 1285–1314) was extremely ambitious and a religious cynic. He outlawed the Knights Templar, an order of the Crusaders, and plundered their treasury in Paris. He also fought with Pope Boniface for authority over spiritual matters. Philip's sons succeeded him, but each of them died in short order. By 1328 his male heirs were all dead. Thus ended a remarkable succession—the Capetian family had managed to keep its lands and title intact for 13 generations.

22. Carolingian Dynasty
European rulers

The union between an aristocratic family and a clerical family created the **Carolingian** dynasty in western Europe. During the seventh century, France was ruled by the Merovingian dynasty. Having closely intermarried for generations, family members were increasingly feeble, both in body and in mind. Therefore, much of the real power was in the hands of the "mayor of the palace." Carolingian **Pepin I**, the first mayor of the palace, married his daughter to the son of Arnulf, the bishop of Metz. The son born to the couple was Pepin II of Heristal (reigned A.D. 687–714).

Pepin of Heristal brought the family to political prominence. His bastard son, **Charles Martel** (reigned A.D. 714–741), defeated the Arabs at the Battle of Tours in A.D. 732 and saved Europe from an Islamic takeover.

The next mayor of the palace, Pepin (III), "the Short" (reigned A.D. 747–768), wrote a long letter to **Pope Zacharias** in Rome. He asked whether the kingdom should be ruled by the person with the title—the Merovingian noble—or by the individual with the real power—the mayor of the palace. After the pope responded in his favor, Pepin sent the last of the Merovingian kings off to a monastery and officially created the new Carolingian dynasty of rulers.

Pepin's two sons, **Charlemagne** and Carloman, fought against each other for control of the dynasty. Charlemagne (reigned A.D. 768–814) prevailed. He united the different regions of France and went on a mission of conquest. Over the next 40 years, Charlemagne conquered Lombardy, Saxony, and much of central Europe, and came to rule more territory than any other European leader until Napoleon Bonaparte. In addition to reigning as king of the Franks, Charlemagne was crowned "Emperor of the Romans" by the pope on Christmas Day in the year A.D. 800.

Louis the Pious (reigned A.D. 814–40) followed his father as king of the Franks and emperor of the Romans. He divided his realm into three parts, to be governed by his sons, Charles the Bald, Lothair, and Louis the German. Their lands approximated present-day France, Germany, and the area between the two countries—Burgundy.

The brothers and their successors fought many wars against each other. Lothair's **"Middle Kingdom"** of Burgundy suffered the most. As a result of this infighting, Charlemagne's empire began to break apart.

Carolingian rule prevailed in Italy until A.D. 901, in Germany until A.D. 911, and in France until A.D. 987 when the **Capet** family replaced the Carolingians. By 1000, the Carolingian dynasty was gone; what emerged from the wreckage of Charlemagne's vast empire was the seed for the creation of the nations of France, Germany, and Italy.

Charlemagne

23. Cato
Roman politicians

Early Rome prided itself on the strength and dignity of its citizens, and few families could point to a more illustrious heritage than the Catos.

Marcus Porcius Cato (234–149 B.C.) was born in Tusculum, Italy, to a lower-class family. Since Roman society was divided between its upper class and the commoners, there seemed little chance for Cato to accomplish great things. However, he caught the attention of a wealthy patron who helped him begin a political career in Rome.

Beginning in 204 B.C. Cato was elected to several important political positions, first as a *quaestor* (low-level magistrate) and eventually rising to the position of *consul*, one of the two ruling magistrates in ancient Rome. Cato's progress through the political ranks was aided immeasurably by his participation in the **Second Punic War** against Carthage and the First Syrian War in Greece.

As he rose in rank and privilege, Cato's distrust of what he saw as the "Hellenization" of the **Roman Empire** increased. Many prominent Romans were bringing in Greek slaves to educate their children and were themselves affecting Greek dress and language. Cato detested this trend toward Hellenic (Greek) culture.

Seeking to remind Romans of their own heritage, Cato wrote his seven-volume

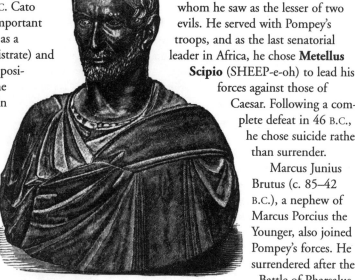

Marcus Junius Brutus

Origines, a history of all the Latin cities. He also became the chief proponent of a third war against **Carthage**. Cato died three years before the destruction of Carthage.

Marcus Porcius the Younger (c. 95–46 B.C.) was a great-grandson of Cato. Beginning in 63 B.C., he made speeches in the Roman Senate against **Julius Caesar** and Gaius Pompey, whom he believed were seeking to turn Rome into a dictatorship.

When the break came between Caesar and Pompey in 49 B.C., Marcus joined the camp of Pompey, whom he saw as the lesser of two evils. He served with Pompey's troops, and as the last senatorial leader in Africa, he chose **Metellus Scipio** (SHEEP-e-oh) to lead his forces against those of Caesar. Following a complete defeat in 46 B.C., he chose suicide rather than surrender.

Marcus Junius Brutus (c. 85–42 B.C.), a nephew of Marcus Porcius the Younger, also joined Pompey's forces. He surrendered after the Battle of Pharsalus and was pardoned by Caesar.

Influenced perhaps by the politics and beliefs of his family, Brutus was one of the chief assassins of Caesar on March 15, 44 B.C. He then went to Greece, and was defeated by the forces of Mark Antony and Octavian (Caesar Augustus); in the aftermath of that defeat, he chose to take his own life.

The Ch'ing family of Chinese emperors came from **Manchuria** in the northeast corner of what is modern-day China.

The family leader of the Ch'ing (meaning "pure") was **Nurhachi** (1559–1626), the chief of the Aisin Goro tribe in Manchuria. He created the "Eight-Banner" system, a military and economic division that cut across tribal lines and reduced tribal rivalries. His son, Abahai, completed the conquest of the other Manchurian tribes. When the **Ming** dynasty collapsed in 1644 from the impact of a peasant rebellion, Abahai's son, Fu-lin, entered the ancient city of **Peking** and was crowned as the first Ch'ing—or *Manchu*—emperor.

During the rules of K'ang Hsi (reigned 1662–1722), Yung Cheng (reigned 1723–35), and Ch'ien Lung (reigned 1736–96), the Ch'ing dynasty reached the apex of its success. K'ang conquered Formosa—present-day Taiwan—in 1683, and Ch'ien acquired **Tibet**, dramatically increasing the vastness of China. By 1790, the Manchu empire of the Ch'ing family exceeded the power of all the earlier Chinese dynasties, with the exception of the **Yuan**.

Ch'ien Lung refused to enter into trade with the European nations. He told a British trade embassy that the Europeans had nothing that he or his people wanted. Chi'en Lung purposely abdicated in favor of his son in 1796, so that his reign would not exceed the 60-year reign of one of his predecessors, **K'ang Hsi**.

The 19th century was much less favorable for the Ch'ing rulers. Advanced European steamboats, rifles, and cannons were used against China in the First and Second Opium Wars. The Ch'ing also faced a tremendous threat from the internal rebellion known as the **Tai-ping**, which began in 1859. The Ch'ing could only subdue the rebellion with the help of Western adventurers.

As the 19th century came to a close, the real power within the Ch'ing family and China as a whole belonged to Tz'u hsi (1835–1908), the regent of the child emperor.

English bomb Canton during first Opium War

She was better known in the West as the "Dowager Empress." Tz'u-hsi conspired with the Chinese "Boxers" in their rebellion against foreigners, but China suffered further humiliation from the Western powers during the **Boxer Rebellion** of 1900.

When Tz'u hsi died, the throne passed to P'u-yi(1906–67), known to westerners as "Henry Pu-Yi." The young emperor was forced to abdicate in 1912 when China became a republic. P'u-yi tried to rule from afar by setting up a court in Japanese-held Manchuria. The Ch'ing dynasty ended when P'u-yi was completely removed from power at the end of World War II.

Through their leadership on the battle-fields and in the halls of government, the Churchills of Great Britain have guided their country through perilous times.

Sir John Churchill (1650–1722), the son of a member of Parliament, married **Sarah Jennings**, who was a lady-in-waiting to Princess Anne, one of the daughters of King James II of England. Churchill rose slowly in society until the **Glorious Revolution** of 1688, in which he supported William III of Orange and Princess Mary in their revolt against King James (see no. 73).

John became captain-general of the English-Dutch army in 1702. He led the combined forces to stunning victories in Germany and Belgium over the armies of King **Louis XIV** of France. He was rewarded with the title of duke of Marlborough.

John Churchill

The next six dukes of Marlborough held seats in Parliament and were esteemed in the nation. The third son of the seventh duke, Lord Randolph Henry Spencer (1849–1895), married an American heiress, Jennie Jerome, in 1874. That same year, she gave birth to their first child—**Winston Leonard Spencer Churchill** (1874-1965).

Randolph appeared to be headed toward a brilliant career in Parliament; however, he developed a severe mental illness and had to resign his post.

Looking to regain the family's fortune and fame, young Winston joined the British army and served in India, the Sudan, and South Africa during the **Boer War**.

Churchill entered Parliament in 1901. He rose to become first lord of the admiralty, serving from 1911 to 1915. After the disastrous British campaign in **Gallipoli,** he resigned his post and spent a number of years in the "political wilderness." During the 1930s, he spoke out strongly against the appeasement of Adolf Hitler by Europe's leaders, particularly by British Prime Minister **Neville Chamberlain**.

The start of World War II brought Churchill to power as Great Britain's prime minister. His tremendous oratorical skills brought him the love and admiration of millions of Britons. He insisted that the British would fight and die on the beaches if necessary, but that they would never surrender to Germany. Once the United States entered the war, Churchill forged a close personal relationship with President Roosevelt that provided the glue to the alliance that defeated Nazi Germany.

Churchill was voted out of office in 1945, but returned as prime minister from 1951 to 1955. He won the **Nobel Prize** for literature in 1953. One of his best-known books was a biography of his famous ancestor, Sir John Churchill. He was made an honorary U.S. citizen by Congress prior to his death.

The Clarks of Virginia were prominent defenders and explorers of the American West. Like many families of their generation, the Clarks were eager to see what lay beyond the Appalachian Mountains.

George Rogers Clark (1752–1818) was born near Charlottesville in what was then the Virginia colony. In 1775 Clark raised an army of settlers to revolt against the proprietors of Kentucky, who wanted it to become the colony of "Transylvania" (part of the Austrian empire). When the **American Revolution** began soon after, Clark turned his attention to the British and Native American foes.

After attacks by **Shawnees** destroyed a number of frontier homes and settlements, Clark secured approval from the state of Virginia to start a military campaign. In the summer of 1778, he led his men in a surprise attack that captured Kaskaskia and Cahokia—both in present-day Illinois—and Vincennes, in present-day Indiana. Through this bold move, Clark captured the British forts that had protected Native American marauders.

British Colonel Henry "the Hair Buyer" Hamilton recaptured Vincennes in December 1778, thereby resuming the threat to the frontier settlements. Clark led 130 men across flooded lands in February, 1779; the attacks caught Hamilton by surprise, and forced the British to surrender. Clark's campaigns in 1778 and 1779 gained much territory for the Americans.

William Clark (1770–1838), a younger brother of George, was born in Caroline County, Virginia. William entered the state militia and served under General "Mad" Anthony Wayne in the **Indian War** of 1794. He retired from the army in 1796 and raised his family near Louisville, Kentucky.

Meriwether Lewis called William out of retirement and asked him to be co-commander of an expedition to find a way to the Pacific Ocean. The team of **Lewis and Clark** left St. Louis, Missouri, on May 14, 1804. They wintered with the Mandan tribe in present-day North Dakota. During the spring and summer of 1805, Lewis and Clark split up and between them explored much of what is today Montana.

In August they joined up again and crossed the **Continental Divide** in the Rocky Mountains. They then built canoes and traveled down the Snake River and finally into the great Columbia River. In November, 1805, the expedition reached the mouth of the Columbia at the Pacific Ocean.

Lewis and Clark's company returned to St. Louis in 1806. Clark, who was the expedition's official cartographer, deserved much of the credit for allowing Americans to envision a nation that stretched from ocean to ocean.

George Rogers Clark

Curie
French scientists

The Curie family of France produced three generations of scientists who made major contributions to the fields of chemistry and physics.

Pierre Curie (1859–1906) was born in Paris. Both his father and grandfather were doctors. He studied physics at the Sorbonne, and by the age of 19, had become a teaching assistant at the Paris Faculty of Sciences.

Pierre met Marie Sklodowska (1867–1934) in 1894. At the time, she was a student at the Sorbonne; when she graduated with her degree in physics, she was ranked first in her class. The couple married in 1895 and worked together for the next 10 years.

Pierre and Marie were inspired by **Henri Becquerel's** discovery that uranium salts emitted rays that resembled X-rays. The Curies searched for other substances that would do the same thing. In 1898, they discovered the new elements polonium—named for Marie's native country, Poland—and radium in the mineral pitchblende

In 1902, the couple performed differential crystallization by separating one-tenth of a gram of radium chloride from a ton of pitchblende. Their work seemed to contradict the principle of the conservation of energy. In 1903 Pierre and Marie shared the **Nobel Prize** in physics with Henri Becquerel.

In 1904 Pierre was named to the chair in physics at the Sorbonne, but his career was tragically cut short in 1906 when he was run over by a truck and killed. Marie continued her work after Pierre's death and was named to his position at the Sorbonne in 1909. She became the first woman to teach there.

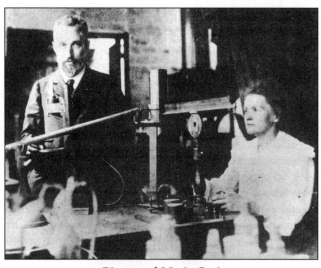

Pierre and Marie Curie

Marie received the Nobel Prize for chemistry in 1911 for her isolation of radium and her studies of its chemical composition. She became the first and only person to ever win Nobel Prizes in both physics and chemistry.

Marie and Pierre's daughter, **Irène Curie** (1897–1956), married **Jean Frédéric Joliot** (1900–58), a student who worked in Marie's laboratory. The couple worked together as intensively as Irène's parents had, and in 1934, they discovered that radioactive isotopes could be artificially created. They shared the Nobel Prize for chemistry in 1935.

During World War II, Frédéric became a leader of the **National Front**, the French resistance movement. After the war, he became high official of the French atomic energy commission, where Irène also served as a commissioner. They were removed from the commission in 1950 because of their communist sympathies. Irène later died of leukemia caused by the handling of radioactive materials.

Frédéric and Irène had two children, Hélène and Pierre. Hélène and her husband became researchers in nuclear physics, while Pierre and his wife specialized in biophysics.

28. Darwin
English scientists

Charles Robert Darwin (1809–82) was only the most famous member of a family that included three generations of scientists, physicians and artists.

Darwin's two grandfathers distinguished themselves in quite different ways. **Erasmus Darwin** (1731–1802) was a physician by training, but he wrote on topics as diverse as botany and erotic poetry. A freethinking radical for his time, Erasmus foreshadowed some of his grandson's ideas about evolution. Darwin's maternal grandfather, Josiah Wedgwood (1730–95), was a noted potter and designer of china.

Doctor Robert Darwin (1766–1848) and Susannah Wedgwood (1765–1817) were Charles's parents. Darwin grew up in a home that epitomized the **Victorian** belief in a divine order to the universe; this belief may have been partly in reaction to the unorthodox views of Erasmus. As a young man, Charles was encouraged by a cousin to pursue his interest in the natural sciences.

In 1831 Charles sailed on the *HMS Beagle* as an unpaid naturalist on a voyage to the **Galapagos Islands** in the Pacific Ocean. He returned from the five-year voyage with a heavy heart because his geological and biological observations had led him to conclude that the Bible must be in error. At that time, biblical scholars believed that the world was approximately 6,000 years old. However, Darwin felt he could prove that it was many, many times older than they thought. How then to account for the relatively recent appearance of humans?

The longer he studied the evidence that he had seen first-hand, the more Darwin came to believe that mankind had slowly evolved in a fashion quite similar to that of other animals. In fact, he determined that humans had probably descended from apes. These findings were reported in his *On the Origin of Species by Means of Natural Selection* (1859) and *The Descent of Man and Selection in Relation to Sex* (1871). Probably no great scientist ever disliked the news he brought as much as Darwin did; much that he had learned disconnected him from the comfortable world view with which he had grown up.

Charles married his first cousin Emma Wedgwood in 1839. They had 10 children, 3 of whom died in infancy. **George Darwin** (1845–1912), their second son, became a noted astronomer. He made pioneering studies of the evolution of the solar system. Francis Darwin (1848–1925) became a botanist. Leonard Darwin (1850–1943), a major in the royal army and an engineer, became a promoter of eugenics, the improvement of humankind through controlled mating. **Horace Darwin** (1851–1928) became a scientific engineer.

Charles Darwin

Three of Joseph DiMaggio, Sr.'s sons—Vincent, Dominic and Joseph, Jr.—became professional baseball players. However, only one rose to the level of a Hall of Famer—and became a world-famous celebrity as well.

Joseph DiMaggio, Sr. and his wife Rosalie emigrated from **Sicily** to the United States in the early 1900s. They settled first in Martinez, California and then moved to San Francisco where Joe Sr. made his living as a fisherman. Joe's second son, **Joseph Paul DiMaggio, Jr.** (1914–99) fell in love with baseball as a youngster. By the time he was 20, he was an outstanding minor league hitter and outfielder with the **San Francisco Seals**, of the Pacific Coast League. In 1936, the **New York Yankees** purchased his contract and brought him up to the majors.

In only Joe's second year—1937—he hit a league-leading 46 home runs. He won the American League batting title twice, with averages of .381 in 1939 and .352 in 1940. His greatest performance was a streak in which he hit safely in 56 consecutive games from May 15 through July 17, 1941. In addition to his hitting, DiMaggio quickly earned the reputation of being the best defensive centerfielder in baseball.

When a rash of injuries forced his retirement in 1951, Joe left baseball with remarkable career statistics: three Most Valuable Player (MVP) awards, 361 home runs and a lifetime batting average of .325. He was inducted into the **Baseball Hall of Fame** in 1955.

Joe's personal life was less happy. After he retired, Joe married actress **Marilyn Monroe**, but the couple filed for divorce a mere nine months after their wedding.

Vincent DiMaggio (1912–86) played with four ball clubs during his 10-year career: Boston, Cincinnati, Pittsburgh, and Philadelphia. Vince played a total of 1,110 games and had a career batting average of .249 with 125 home runs.

Dominic Paul DiMaggio (b. 1917) was called the "Little Professor" by his teammates because he was one of the few ballplayers to wear glasses. He played for 11 seasons with the Boston Red Sox. Dominic excelled in his role as leadoff hitter and was a talented center fielder as well. He retired with a lifetime batting average of .298 and 87 home runs in a total of 1,399 games.

Although all three men were excellent ballplayers, it was Joe's skill and style that captivated the public. For the rest of his life, Joe DiMaggio remained the ideal American hero: a child of immigrants whose hard work and determination became an inspiration to millions.

Joe Di Maggio

30. Du Pont
Politicians and industrialists

Along with the family fortune, the Du Ponts have built a reputation for excellence and innovation in the chemical and plastics industries.

Pierre-Samuel Du Pont de Nemours (1739–1817) was born in France. Trained as an economist, he played a leading role in the early days of the **French Revolution** by twice serving as president of the Revolutionary Legislature—the Constituent Assembly. He made his first trip to America in 1799, and

E. I. Du Pont

then settled there permanently in 1815.

His son Eleuthère Irénée Du Pont (1771–1834) founded the family's fortunes. He established a company near Wilmington, Delaware to make gunpowder for both military and sporting uses. By 1830 the company employed 140 people and produced 800,000 barrels of gunpowder annually.

Victor-Marie Du Pont (1767–1827), Eleuthère's older brother, served as a French diplomat to the United States; in 1800 he settled in America, where he managed his brother's woolen mills. Victor's son, Samuel Francis Du Pont (1803–65), served as a naval officer in both the Mexican War and the Civil War.

Alfred Victor Du Pont (1798–1856) was Eleuthère's oldest son. He created a new chemical used in making gunpowder, and his fortunes soared with the demand for gunpowder during the Mexican War. His younger brother, Henry Du Pont (1812–89), ran the family business from 1850 until 1889. Under his leadership, the business began making dynamite, and provided four million pounds of gunpowder to the Union army during the Civil War.

Henry Algernon Du Pont (1838–1926), the oldest son of Henry Du Pont, graduated first in his class at the U.S. Military Academy at **West Point** and served with distinction in the Civil War. He was also the U.S. senator from Delaware from 1906 to 1917.

Another of Alfred's grandsons, Thomas Coleman (1863–1930), was president of the family firm from 1902 until 1915. He went on to serve as the U.S. senator from Delaware from 1921 to 1922 and 1925 to 1928.

Pierre Samuel Du Pont (1870–1954), also a grandson of Alfred Victor, headed the family company from 1915 to 1919. During that time, the firm supplied 1.3 billion pounds of smokeless gunpowder to the Allied armies during World War I. The number of Du Pont employees rose from 5,300 to around 85,000, and Pierre Samuel introduced the use of new chemicals. In the 1920s, the company entered the plastics business.

Pierre Samuel Du Pont IV (b. 1935) served as a congressman from Delaware from 1971 until 1977 and as governor of the state from 1977 until 1985.

Aaron Burr

The Edwards family produced two famous public servants, Jonathan Edwards and Aaron Burr. Although they were related by blood, their impacts on American history were quite different.

Jonathan Edwards (1703–58) was born in East Windsor, Connecticut. He married Sarah Pierpont and the couple settled in the town of Northampton, Massachusetts, where Edwards was ordained into the **Puritan** ministry in 1727.

During the 1730s and 1740s, he became the foremost leader of the **Great Awakening**, a religious revival movement. Edwards preached his most famous sermon, "Sinners in the Hands of an Angry God," in Enfield, Connecticut in 1741. In the sermon, he likened God's relationship to mankind as that of a human being holding a loathsome insect over the fireplace. It was hardly a comforting image to his congregation. In 1750, they voted to dismiss him from his post.

Edwards and his family moved to Stockbridge, Massachusetts where they served as missionaries to the **Native Americans**.

They lived in poverty until 1758, when Edwards was named the first president of the College of New Jersey (modern-day Princeton University). Soon after his arrival in New Jersey, Edwards was inoculated for smallpox. Unfortunately, he received too high a dose and he died.

Aaron Burr (1756–1836) was a grandson of Edwards. He graduated from Princeton College in 1772 and served with distinction in the Revolutionary War.

Burr was attorney general in 1789 and later elected to the U.S. Senate where he served from 1791 to 1797. He ran unsuccessfully for president in 1796 and 1800, although he actually tied Thomas Jefferson in the electoral vote in the 1800 election. Burr lost the election, when the U.S. House of Representatives voted for Jefferson. Burr served as Jefferson's vice president from 1801 to 1805.

In 1804, Burr challenged **Alexander Hamilton** to a duel over Hamilton's published remarks about his character. Burr shot and killed Hamilton at Weehawken, New Jersey, on July 11, 1804.

After Burr served the remaining months of his vice presidency, he departed for the Northwest Territory (present-day Ohio, Indiana, and Illinois). Over the next two years, he engaged in many mysterious activities; his enemies charged that he intended to lead a group of supporters in a scheme to bring about a secession of American western territory. In 1807, Burr was arrested and taken to Virginia, where he was tried for treason.

Chief Justice **John Marshall** presided over the trial and found insufficient evidence against Burr. Acquitted on all counts, Burr left the country for Europe. Burr returned penniless to New York City in 1812 and practiced law there for the rest of his life.

The Eliot family led the way in education, landscape architecture, and poetry for several generations.

Samuel Atkins Eliot (1798–1862), was a prominent Massachusetts politician. As mayor of Boston, encouraged the musical life of the city, and was renowned for bailing many paupers out of the local debtor's prison.

His son, **Charles William Eliot** (1834–1926), attended Harvard College where he studied chemistry. In 1869, he became president of his alma mata —now Harvard University—and remained in that position for 40 years. Having traveled in Europe, he admired the European style of education, and brought the elective system to Harvard. This allowed students to choose their own courses instead of following a set program in the classics. Eliot also became known as a counselor to American presidents. Woodrow Wilson offered him the ambassadorship to Great Britain, but Eliot declined.

Charles Eliot (1859–97), the oldest son of Charles William, found his vocation in landscape architecture. He worked with Frederick Law Olmsted, the creator of American-style landscape architecture, and was instrumental in founding the Massachusetts Trust of Public Reservations in 1891. Charles's untimely death led his father to ask younger brother, Samuel, to renounce his ministry and enter landscape architecture, but he refused the request.

William Eliot

Charles William's grandson **Thomas Hopkinson Eliot** (1907–91) was one of the leaders of the "Brain Trust" of President Franklin D. Roosevelt's New Deal in the 1930s. He was a co-author of the Social Security Act, which gave some measure of financial security to millions of Americans.

Thomas Stearns (T.S.) Eliot (1888–1965), a fifth cousin, was born in St. Louis, Missouri. He studied at Harvard and went to England to pursue his career, first in banking and then in publishing. He became the most renowned poet of his time; among his most famous works is "The Waste Land" (1922), which many people consider to be the finest expression of the desolation that World War I wrought upon his generation. He received the **Nobel Prize** for literature in 1948.

Samuel Eliot Morison (1887–1976), a distant cousin, was a maritime historian. Among his many books, he wrote about the adventures of such explorers as Samuel Champlain and Christopher Columbus. No armchair historian, Morison sailed many of the same routes as his historical heroes; he accompanied the U.S. Navy in its invasion of North Africa in 1942. Morison later wrote the definitive multivolume history of the U.S. Navy's actions during World War II.

33. Ericson
Norwegian explorers

One of the great sea-venturing families in history, the Ericsons led the exploration of North America. The first family leader was Eric Thorvaldson Rauda (c. A.D. 950–1000), known as **"Eric the Red."** Born in Jaeren, Norway, Eric emigrated to Iceland in the A.D. 970s when his father, Thorvald, was exiled from his homeland for committing several murders.

Eric married and his wife Thjodhild had two children, Lief and Thornstein. When Eric was banished from Iceland for committing the same crimes as his father had, he set sail with his family for a land 200 miles to the west—a land that could be seen from Iceland's mountains on a clear day. Eric named it **Greenland** to entice future colonists.

Eric the Red

Eric returned to Iceland, and in 986, sailed again to Greenland with 25 shiploads of colonists. Only 14 of the ships reached their destination; the other 11 were driven back by storms or disappeared without a trace. Eric directed the building of settlements on the southwest shore of Greenland.

His son, Lief Ericson (c. A.D. 970–1020), sailed from Greenland to Norway in A.D. 999. There he met King Olaf Tryggvason (see no. 47), who tried to convert him to Christianity. Lief returned to Greenland in 1000, and one year later, he sailed west to discover new lands. Eric gave his consent, but not his full blessing, to the venture.

Led by Lief, the Greenlanders discovered three new lands, which they named Helluland, Markland, and Vinland (Wineland). It is very likely that these three lands were modern-day Baffin Island, Labrador, and Newfoundland. Lief and his fellow explorers wintered in Vinland before returning to Greenland the following year. There he became known as **"Lief the Lucky"** for his successful explorations.

Thorvald Ericson (c. A.D. 975–c. 1004), Lief's younger brother, sailed from Greenland in 1003 in search of Vinland. When he and his crew arrived, they created a settlement where they spent the next two winters. Thorvald was killed while fighting a native people he called the "Skraelings," either members of the Beothuk tribe of present-day Newfoundland or the Micmacs of Nova Scotia. The remainder of Thorvald's crew returned to Greenland.

The Ericson family exemplified the **Norse** seafaring tradition. From Eric to Thorvald, the family members drew an arc of voyages and settlements from Scandinavia to Iceland, Greenland, and the New World. Though **Christopher Columbus** was the European who is credited with discovering a "New World," there is little doubt that the intrepid Ericsons preceded him by almost 500 years.

For nearly two centuries, members of the Field family have made major contributions to American life. Though there are many branches of the family, those from Stockbridge and Conway, Massachusetts, are especially notable.

Cyrus West Field (1819–92) was born in Stockbridge. At the age of 15, he left home to seek his fortune in New York City. He began work as an errand boy in a dry goods firm; by the time he was in his early 30s, he had made his fortune in the manufacturing business.

Successful enough to retire at the age of 33, Cyrus turned his attention to other areas. Interested in improved methods of communication, he pushed the idea of laying a telegraph cable across the **Atlantic Ocean**, and he promoted it aggressively. In 1857 a copper cable was laid that connected southern Ireland with Newfoundland—a distance of 1,950 miles. On August 16, 1857, **Queen Victoria** sent a message of congratulations to President James Buchanan through the new cable.

Two older brothers of Cyrus pursued the law. **Stephen Johnson Field** (1816–99) sat on the U.S. Supreme Court from 1863 until 1897, thereby breaking the longevity record set by Chief Justice John Marshall. David Dudley Field (1805–94) drafted an international law code in 1872.

Marshall Field (1834–1906) was born in Conway, Massachusetts. Like his cousin Cyrus, he went to work in the dry goods business, first in Pittsfield, Massachusetts, then in Chicago, Illinois. Marshall rose from clerk to general manager of a local department store, and in 1881 he reorganized it as Marshall Field & Company.

Marshall became a philanthropist in his later years. He donated an initial $1 million to the **Chicago World's Fair** that grew to a far greater sum. He also established the Field Museum of Natural History in Chicago and a library in his hometown.

Marshall Field III (1893–1956) was a grandson of the department store's founder. Born in Chicago, he became an ardent supporter of President Franklin D. Roosevelt's New Deal. He championed social reforms and child welfare and established the Field Foundation.

Marshal III turned to publishing and founded the *Chicago Sun* newspaper in 1941, which later became the morning *Sun-Times*. He also consolidated all his publishing activities, including book publishing house Simon & Schuster, into Field Enterprises.

Marshall Field IV (1916–65) was the son of Marshall III. After serving in the U.S. Navy during World War II, he joined the staff of the *Chicago Sun*. He later became president of Field Enterprises, and in 1959 he bought the *Chicago Daily News*.

Marshall Field

Three generations of Fondas have graced the American stage and screen. **Henry Fonda** (1905-1982) was born in Grand Island, Nebraska. He briefly attended the University of Minnesota before he went to New York City. Fonda made his **Broadway** debut in *The Farmer Takes a Wife* in 1934, and then starred in the movie version a year later.

Fonda quickly became a major star. His

Jane and Henry Fonda

self-effacing manner and dry delivery gave American audiences what they wanted in a movie star: decency, modesty, and enough gumption to defeat the bad guys. He appeared in more than 100 films; among his most famous roles were the depression-era, idealistic farm worker Tom Joad in the adaptation of **John Steinbeck's** classic novel, *The Grapes of Wrath* (1940), His last film appearance, *On Golden Pond* (1981)—in which he costarred with **Katherine Hepburn** and his daughter Jane—brought him an Academy Award for best actor.

Henry had two children from his second marriage, to Francis Seymour Brokaw. Jane Fonda (b. 1937), dropped out of Vassar College and worked briefly as a model. She made her Broadway debut in *There Was a Little Girl* (1960), and her film debut in *Tall Story* (1960).

Fonda won the Academy Award for best actress for her roles in *Klute* (1971) and *Coming Home* (1978). In the latter film, she addressed an issue close to her heart, the **Vietnam War**. Supporters of the war condemned her and nicknamed her "Hanoi Jane" when she vigorously protested U.S. involvement in Vietnam by traveling to North Vietnam and speaking out against the United States.

In 1980, she began a new career with a series of exercise videos, and she became one of the top spokespersons for aerobic exercise regimens. After failed marriages to French film director Roger Vadim and California politician Tom Hayden, Jane married media mogul Ted Turner, founder of CNN and owner of the Atlanta Braves baseball team.

Jane's brother, **Peter Fonda** (b. 1940), bore a strong resemblance to their father. Peter made his film debut in *Tammy and the Doctor* (1963), but his greatest success was the film *Easy Rider* (1969), which he co-wrote, produced, and starred in. Nearly thirty years later, Peter was nominated for an Oscar for his leading role in *Ulee's Gold.*

Peter's daughter, **Bridget Fonda** (b. 1964), made her film debut in *Partners* (1982). By 1993 she had become one of Hollywood's busiest actresses. Her films include *It Could Happen to You* (1994), *Jackie Brown* (1997), and *A Simple Plan* (1998).

36. Ford
American industrialists

If there is one American family most responsible for making the automobile a central part of the American way of life, it is the Fords of Michigan.

The son of a farmer, **Henry Ford** (1863–1947) was born near Dearborn, Michigan. He attended school until the age of 15, when he became a machinist's apprentice in Detroit. When he was in his late 20s, he began to experiment with different types of engines. By the age of 30, he was chief engineer of the Edison Illuminating Company in Detroit, but he had ideas of his own. By 1896, Ford had built his first automobile; in 1899, he quit his secure job and founded the short-lived Detroit Automobile Company. That firm went out of business the following year, but three years later, Ford raised $100,000 from investors, and went on to establish the **Ford Motor Company**.

Using standardized parts and assembly-line methods, Ford eventually turned out millions of cars for average Americans, beginning with the black, 4-cylinder, 20-horsepower **Model T** in 1908. Ford specialized in "mass production," that enabled him to offer his cars for very reasonable prices; by 1913, he was able to sell the Model T for only $500.

Henry Ford and son, Edsel

Edsel Bryant Ford (1893–1943), was Henry's only child. In 1919 he became head of Ford Motor Company in name, although the real power remained with his father, who that year had bought out all the remaining stockholders so he could have complete control over the company. Over the next 20 years, Henry became increasingly rigid and authoritarian, and as a businessman, he innovated less and less; eventually his company fell behind in the field of auto innovation. Two years after the untimely death of his son, he finally retired and yielded the running of the company to his grandson, Henry Ford II.

Henry Ford II (1917–87) served in the U.S. Navy during World War II and returned home to find himself named president of Ford Motor Company. Ford soon showed that his managerial talents were equal to the great mechanical abilities of his grandfather.

Ford swiftly fired the "company police" his father had hired, settled a labor dispute, and reorganized the company. Between 1930 and 1941, the company's share of the cars manufactured in America had dropped from 40 percent to less than 20 percent, but Henry II reversed the trend. Ford surpassed **Chrysler Corporation** to become the second largest car manufacturer in 1953. A string of important car design successes throughout the decades of the late 20th century—the Ford **Mustang,** Mercury Cougar, and Lincoln Continental—have kept Ford among the "Big Three" automobile manufacturers of the United States.

The Fugger banking family thrived during the late Middle Ages and during the Renaissance before their fortunes ran aground on the rocky politics of the Protestant Reformation in the 16th century.

Hans Fugger (1348–1408) was born in Graben, Swabia (modern-day Germany). He established the Fugger family in Augsburg around 1367. A wool weaver, he moved up in the world through two consecutive marriages to daughters of local weaving guild members. He left a modest estate to his two sons, Andreas and Jakob; however, it was two of Hans' grandsons who increased the family's fortunes.

Two of Jakob's sons, Ulrich (1441–1510) and Georg (1453–1506), expanded the family's international trade business. They began to compete with the strong merchant organization of cities, called the **Hanseatic League**, on the Baltic Sea. With the aid of their brother Markus in Rome, they helped with the sale of church indulgences, documents which promised forgiveness for sins.

The youngest of the seven sons, Jakob (1459–1525), later called "Jakob the Rich," brought the family business into its full flower. He moved to **Innsbruck** (modern-day Austria) in 1485 and concentrated on the silver and copper trade. Jakob took full command of the family firm in 1510. He acquired mines in Hungary, invested in Spain and its trade in the Americas, and entered the spice trade.

Jakob financed the election of **Charles Hapsburg** (see no. 46) as Holy Roman Emperor in 1519. Jakob alone raised 544,000 of the 852,000 guilders required to bribe the electors. Having thus made allegiance with the Hapsburg family, Jakob never changed course. He loaned enormous sums to Emperor Charles V.

Jakob's nephew, **Anton Fugger** (1493–1560), continued the policy, making loans to King Philip II of Spain and Emperor

Charles V visiting Anton Fugger

Ferdinand I. These loans were vital to the Hapsburg families. Through this money, they financed the wars that kept the Catholic **Holy Roman Empire** from falling to the Protestants.

These loans were disastrous for the Fuggers, however. Anton witnessed the default of one debt after another by the Spanish and Austrian Hapsburgs. Anton considered closing the family business entirely, but it continued in a limited fashion for a century after his death.

It is no exaggeration to state that the Genghisid dynasty held more power and controlled more land than any other rulers in the history of the world.

Temüjin, better known as **Genghis Khan** (c. 1162–1227), was the son of Yesugei, chief of a Mongol tribe. Because of his extraordinary skill in diplomacy and battle, the Mongols came to call him "Genghis Khan," or supreme leader. He was perhaps the most ferocious conqueror the world has ever known. During his reign (1206-1227), the Mongols invaded China, capturing the capital of Peking from the **Chin Empire**, destroyed the Kharismian Empire of present-day Afghanistan and Iran, defeated a large army in Kiev in north Russia, and conducted a successful invasion of Moslem cities in northern India.

Genghis Khan had several wives, the most important of whom was Borte. Borte gave birth to four sons: Jochi, Chagatai, Ögödei, and Tolui. Surprisingly, Jochi and his descendants never took the throne as Khaghan (Great Khan) after the death of Temüjin. Never insisting on the throne for themselves, they were influential in deciding what other member of the family would occupy it.

Ögödei (reigned 1229–41) became Great Khan after the death of his father. An effective military leader, he was known for his consumption of alcohol and drunken rages. During his years in power, the Mongols continued their conquests, fighting against southern China.

Kuyuk (reigned 1246–48), the son of Ögödei, followed his father as leader for only two years. After Kuyuk's death, leadership passed to the children of Tolui and his remarkable wife, Sorghaghtani Beki. She groomed each of her children for leadership, and through an alliance with Batu, the son of Jochi, she outmaneuvered the other family

Kublai Khan

branches. Her son Mongke became Great Khan in 1251.

During Mongke's rule, the Mongols planned the final destruction of the southern Chinese (Sung) empire. Mongke ruled until his death in 1259, when his younger brother **Kublai** (reigned 1260–94) won the struggle for succession. Kublai led the Mongol people to their greatest victories. He overcame the Sung Empire and sent his forces even farther south to attack Annam and Burma. By the time of his death, he was weary of the throne. He left no successors vigorous enough to continue his conquests.

Chagatai's descendants became the Khans of Transoxiania in western Asia, with Samarqand as their capital. The descendants of Jochi and Batu became the Khans of the Golden Horde in Russia. Kublai's descendants formed the **Yuan** dynasty that ruled all of China until 1370. Hulegu (1217–65), one of Kublai's brothers, passed his leadership as Khan of present-day Iran to his descendants.

The tremendous wealth of the Getty family began in the American oil fields.

George Franklin Getty (c. late 1800s–1930), the founder of the family fortunes, began his career as an insurance lawyer in Minneapolis, Minnesota. Hired to investigate a claim in the **Oklahoma Territory**, he soon became fascinated by the thriving oil business. Getty, moved family—his wife, Sarah, and their only child, Jean Paul—to Oklahoma, where he founded and developed George F. Getty Oil, Inc.

J. Paul Getty I

well there in 1953, and by 1957, Getty had become the single richest man in the United States; his wealth was estimated at well over $1 billion. A devoted art collector, he used some of his vast wealth to open the **J. Paul Getty Museum** in Malibu, California, in 1953.

Getty married and divorced five times and had five sons. The oldest, George F. Getty (1924–1973), was his father's favorite. He served as vice president of **Getty Oil** until his

While George prospered in the oil business, Jean Paul (1892–1976) attended several preparatory schools and colleges before he graduated from Oxford University in England in 1913. He then went to Oklahoma and entered the oil business as a wildcatter, (driller) in association with his father. By 1915, Jean Paul had made his first million dollars.

Jean Paul inherited an estate valued at $15 million upon his father's death in 1930. He was therefore well-positioned to take advantage of the economic crash of the **Great Depression**. Using his cash reserves, he bought up oil shares at cheap prices. After his acquisition of Tidewater Association Oil Company in 1937, Getty expanded his business in several areas. Tidewater processed and sold oil in the United States while Getty Oil expanded overseas.

The great coup in Getty's career was his opening of oil fields in the "Neutral Zone" located between Saudi Arabia and Kuwait on the Arabian peninsula. He opened his first

death. The other sons—J. Ronald, J.Paul II, Gordon, and Timothy, played almost no role in the operation of the family business; however, all four were able to draw substantial amounts of money from the huge family trust and live very comfortable lives.

In 1973, the family faced a crisis when **Jean Paul Getty III**, Jean Paul's grandson, was kidnapped by terrorists in Rome. The American public was shocked when Jean Paul refused to pay the ransom for his return. After the young man's severed ear was delivered as proof that the kidnappers meant business, his grandfather paid the $750,000 ransom. Jean Paul III was released after six months of captivity.

Jean Paul Getty died in 1976 at Sutton Place, his estate near **London**. His son Gordon—who served as co-trustee of the family trust until 1985—sold all the Getty oil holdings to Texaco for $9.98 billion in 1984. The following year, the trust was divided into six equally-sized trusts that continue to sustain the family members.

"All love is sweet," Percy Bysshe Shelley wrote in *Prometheus Unbound* (1818). Ironically, love contributed greatly to the saga of heartbreak, despair, and tragedy that became the hallmark of the Godwin and Shelley family of romantic poets and writers.

William Godwin (1756–1836) began a career as a minister, moved to London, and became a journalist and political writer. His *Enquiry Concerning Political Justice* (1793) was a landmark study; Godwin wrote the book as a rebuttal to Edmund Burke's denunciation of the French Revolution.

Mary Wollstonecraft (1759–97) worked as a publisher's assistant in London. Deeply inspired by the French Revolution, she nevertheless found it insufficient; therefore, she wrote *Vindication of the Rights of Woman* (1792), which was the strongest feminist tract until that time.

Mary went to Paris and met Gilbert Imlay, an American adventurer. The two had one daughter, Fanny Imlay. When Mary lost interest in Imlay, she tried unsuccessfully to kill herself.

After she recovered, Mary met Godwin. The radical philosopher and the feminist married in 1797. Later that year, Mary died days after giving birth to their daughter, **Mary Wollstonecraft Godwin** (1797-1851).

In 1814, Mary met the young poet, **Percy Bysshe Shelley** (1792–1822). Raised in luxury, the son of a baronet, Shelley was an atheist with revolutionary political beliefs, and his ideas and behavior left him alienated from his family. Nevertheless, he displayed great literary talent at an early age.

Although he was married to a woman named **Harriet Westbrook** and had two children at the time, Percy eloped with Mary and left his family. When they returned to England they learned that Mary's stepsister Fanny had poisoned herself in a fit of depression. In December, 1816, tragedy struck again when Percy's wife, Harriet, drowned herself. Shelley quickly married Mary, hoping the gesture of respectability would win him custody of his two children by Harriet. The effort failed.

During this period, Shelley wrote some of his most well-known works, including *The Revolt of Islam*, a portion of *Rosalind and Helen*, and other poems.

During this time of extreme family distress, Mary Shelley wrote the gothic novel *Frankenstein*. Published in 1818, the book became an immediate success. Her depiction of a scientist who gave life to a horrible monster was seen later by many as a prediction of the **Industrial Revolution.**

Percy and Mary had three children, William, Clara, and Percy Florence; William and Clara died at a very young age, while Percy survived his father. Percy and Mary and their children moved to **Italy** in 1818. He drowned in a storm at sea off the Italian coast in 1822; Mary lived for nearly another 30 years.

Percy Bysshe Shelley

41. Gracchus
Roman politicians

During the second century B.C., the Roman Gracchus family exemplified personal virtue and public leadership.

The family belonged to the upper class. **Tiberius Gracchus** (c. 210–154 B.C.), a Roman politician, married Cornelia, daughter of Scipio Africanus, hero of the Second Punic War. The couple had twelve children, six boys and six girls.

When Tiberius died, his widow received many attractive offers of marriage. She declined all the invitations, citing her need to care for her children and see to their education. Cornelia's two sons, Tiberius and Gaius, followed their father into politics.

Tiberius Gracchus II (c. 163–133 B.C.) was appalled by the unfair distribution of land and wealth. Huge amounts of Italian land had been concentrated into *latifundia,* estates held by wealthy Romans. Meanwhile, the average Italian farmers, who had borne the brunt of the Punic Wars, had lost their land and been forced to become city dwellers, often living in poverty.

Tiberius served as a *quaestor* (judge) in 137 B.C. and was elected as one of the empire's 10 tribunes in 133 B.C. Tribunes could press for new laws, and also had the authority to veto any legislation under consideration in the **Roman Senate**. Tiberius introduced a bill to the Senate that limited the amount of public land any one citizen could possess. One of his fellow tribunes, **Octavius**, vetoed the measure. Tiberius had Octavius deposed and set up a three-man commission—himself, his brother, and his father-in-law—to look into land settlements and compensation for farmers.

Tiberius' ideas were strongly opposed by the large landowners. When he ran for re-election as tribune, his powerful opponents organized a plot against him. A riot ensued, and Tiberius and many of his followers were killed. Intent on stifling Tiberius's reforms permanently, the Senate condemned many of his remaining supporters to death.

Tiberius's death was seen as martyrdom to the cause of the public good. His younger brother, **Gaius Gracchus** (153–121 B.C.), was elected a quaestor in 126 B.C. and then a tribune in 124 B.C. Like his brother, Gaius was also strongly in favor of land reform. He sponsored a grain law that would offer low grain prices to the average Roman citizen. When Gaius moved to give Roman citizenship to all Italians, the conservative forces took action against him. Gaius was killed in the streets of Rome and 3,000 of his followers were put to death.

Cornelia proudly declared she would rather be known as "the mother of the Gracchi brothers than as the daughter of **Scipio Africanus.**" Her noble stance and the public deeds of her sons were among the last efforts to keep Rome a true republic.

Gaius Gracchus being chased

One of the most colorful—and certainly one of the longest-lived royal families—is the Royal House of Monaco, the Grimaldis. The tiny principality of **Monaco** (just 0.7 square miles in size) was ruled first by the Holy Roman Empire and then by the Italian city of **Genoa**. In 1297 Rainier I, Grimaldi, took the throne of an independent Monaco.

For the next 13 generations, the Grimaldi family ruled the principality. The 13th generation of Grimaldi rulers ended with the death of Princess Louise-Hippolyte in 1731. Her husband, the **Count of Thorigny** of the Matignon family, followed her as ruler. He chose to take the name Grimaldi, and after his death the throne went to their son, Prince Honore III.

The family was ousted from power during the French Revolution, but they returned with Prince Honore IV (reigned 1814–1841). Prince Albert (reigned 1889–1922) divorced his first wife, who was English, in order to marry Alice Heine of New Orleans, Louisiana. She became the first—but not the last—American princess of Monaco. She brought opera and ballet to its "pleasure city," **Monte Carlo**, and was instrumental in putting Monaco "on the map" with sophisticated and wealthy travelers.

The reign of Prince Louis II (1922-1949) was thick with troubles. When Germany occupied France during World War II, he chose to align himself with the pro-Nazi Vichy government. Because of his collaboration with the fascists, the citizens of Monaco were delighted to see Louis's reign end in 1949, and the throne pass to his grandson, Prince **Rainier III** (b. 1923).

Handsome, ambitious, and determined to see his principality thrive, Prince Rainier encouraged foreign corporations to make Monaco their headquarters by offering them a tax haven. In 1954 he married the Academy

Rainier and Grace with Caroline

Award–winning American movie actress **Grace Kelly** from Philadelphia. The wedding was a tremendous celebrity affair. The royal couple had three children, Princess Caroline (b. 1957), Prince Albert (b. 1958), and Princess Stephanie (b. 1965).

The charmed life of the royal family changed after 1982. That year, Princess Grace died from injuries suffered in an auto accident. **Princess Caroline** divorced her first husband, Philippe Junot, and married Stefano Casiraghi in 1983. They had three children— Andrea, Charlotte, and Pierre. Stefano's life ended in a boating accident in 1990. The tragedy of these deaths cast a pall over the royal family, and its previous fairytale existence.

Nonetheless, the family endures. After 13 generations of the Grimaldi family and 8 generations of the Matignon-Grimaldi line, it is hard to envision a different family sitting on the throne of the second-smallest sovereign state in the world.

43. Grimké
American abolitionists

The Grimké family played a major role in exposing the great evils perpetrated by the slave system in the United States.

John Faucheraud Grimké (1752–1819) was born in Charles Town— later Charleston—South Carolina. Of French and German ancestry, he served with distinction with the Americans during the Revolutionary War. He then became a prominent legislator and magistrate in South Carolina. A slave-holder himself, Grimké was known as a stern and unbending judge, who took very seriously the sanctity of private property—which he and most South Carolinians believed included slaves.

Grimké married Mary Smith in 1784. The couple had 14 children, 4 of whom distinguished themselves in public life.

Thomas Smith Grimké (1786–1834) became a noted pacifist in South Carolina. He supported the temperance movement and promoted the idea that American slaves should be set free to create their own colonies in Africa. **Frederick Grimké** (1791–1863) became a judge and a political theorist. He moved to Ohio and sat on the bench of the state supreme court from 1836 to 1842.

Two of the Grimké sisters, Sarah Moore (1792–1873) and Angelina Emily (1805–79), attracted the most public attention in their lifetimes. They joined the Society of Friends—**the Quakers**—and moved north to Philadelphia.

Angelina wrote to publisher and noted abolitionist **William Lloyd Garrison** in 1835; much to her surprise, he published the letter in his abolitionist journal, The *Liberator*. Encouraged by Garrison's reception, Angelina persuaded her sister to accompany her in making public speeches on the issue. The sisters made their first public appearance in Philadelphia in 1835; almost from the start, they found warm and sympathetic audiences.

In 1836 they moved to **New York** and spoke before ever-larger audiences. The opposition of religious leaders to their popularity prompted them to add women's rights to their list of causes.

Around this time, the sisters managed to persuade their mother to give the family slaves to them as their share of the family property. The sisters immediately freed the slaves.

Angelina also wrote a pamphlet entitled *Appeal to the Christian Women of the South* in 1836. She and Sarah continued to publicly speak out on this slavery issue until 1838. In that year, Angelina married **Theodore D. Weld** (1803–95), a noted abolitionist, and the couple and Sarah moved to Boston. The sisters stopped making appearances due to Angelina's health, but the energy created by their speeches spread to other advocates of abolition. Angelina, her husband, and her sister lived together in Hyde Park, Massachusetts for the remainder of their lives.

Sarah Moore Grimké

Few pairs of brothers have affected the lives of millions of children—and adults—to the extent of folklorists **Jacob Ludwig Carl Grimm** (1785–1863) and **Wilhelm Carl Grimm** (1786–1859).

The brothers were the two oldest children of Philipp Wilhelm Grimm, a lawyer, who died in 1796. They grew up in Hanau, in the principality of Hesse-Cassel, **Germany**. Inseparable from an early age, they went to school together in Cassel, then went to Marburg to study law from 1802 to 1806. They originally planned to follow in their father's footsteps and practice law, but they were increasingly drawn to older forms of German literature, in particular peasant stories.

While they worked by day—Jacob was a librarian at Cassel, Wilhelm worked as a secretary—they continued their private research. They found an enormous treasure trove of stories that existed mostly in oral form and were passed down by parents to their children over many generations. Determined to preserve their findings, the brothers took 10 years to write and edit *Kinder-un Hausmarchen*, better known to Americans as *Grimm's Fairy Tales*; the stories were published between 1812 and 1822. By studying this elusive form of literature, the brothers founded the new discipline of folklore.

Jacob went on to write the four-volume *Deutsche Grammatik* between 1819 and 1837. In this masterful four-volume work, he examined far more than German grammar. He developed a theory about the use of consonant sounds that showed similarity between a number of Germanic languages. This led to the formulation of **Grimm's Law**, a description of the set of changes that certain sounds underwent in the development of the German language. The importance of this law demonstrates the principle of language that sound

Grimm brothers

change is a regular phenomenon, and not a random process.

The brothers moved to **Göttingen**, Germany, in 1829. They both became professors at the university there, but they lost their positions after they became involved in a political protest. Exiled from Göttingen, they went to **Berlin** in 1840 and continued to work together on folkloric and linguistic studies. Their mutual devotion to their work never wavered.

Wilhelm and Jacob left behind an immense collection of stories that have become part of European and American literature, including *Hansel and Gretel, Cinderella, Snow White* and *Rumpelstiltskin*. Even if some of the characters have been altered in the retelling on television and in films, the strength of the stories remains indelible. This might not have been, if two brothers had not spent their lives preserving them for future generations.

Guggenheim
American industrialists and philanthropists

Daniel Guggenheim

The riches to be found underneath American soil built the mining industry and the fortunes of the Guggenheim family.

Meyer Guggenheim (1828–1905) was born in Langnau, Switzerland. He grew up in a small Jewish ghetto and wanted a life with greater opportunity. He boarded a ship for the United States at the age of 19, and on the voyage he met his future wife, Barbara Myers. The couple settled in New York City, where Guggenheim worked for the next 20 years, primarily importing Swiss embroidered materials.

Guggenheim changed his business focus around 1890. He went west to **Colorado** and began mining and smelting copper. He formed the Guggenheim Exploration Company in 1899. In 1901, he carried out a business coup by winning the leadership of the American Smelting and Refining Company. He then retired from the business, leaving it to his eight sons and three daughters.

Meyer's son **Daniel Guggenheim** (1856–1930) spent his early working years in Switzerland, learning the embroidery business. He returned to the United States and entered the copper and smelting business. He became the guiding force of the **American Smelting and Refining Company**, serving as president from 1901 until 1919. He pioneered its expansion from Alaska all the way to Chile.

Daniel's brother, **Simon Guggenheim** (1867–1941), went to Colorado in 1892 and worked in the family mining business. Fascinated by the West, he remained in Colorado and represented the state in the U.S. Senate as a Republican from 1907 to 1913. After Daniel's retirement, Simon went to New York City and served as president of the American Smelting and Refining Company until his death.

Solomon Robert Guggenheim (1861–1949), the fourth of Meyer's eight sons, also studied in Switzerland. He returned to the United States in 1889 and expanded the family's business operations in Mexico. He joined the board of directors in 1901 and founded the **Yukon Gold Company** in Alaska. Solomon retired in 1919 and followed his passion, art collecting. He established the Solomon Robert Guggenheim Foundation for the promotion of art. He commissioned Frank Lloyd Wright to design and build the Solomon R. Guggenheim Museum in New York City; the museum houses one of the world's great collections of modern art.

Peggy Guggenheim (1898–1979), a niece of Solomon, led a bohemian lifestyle, first in New York City, then in Paris where she collected fine art. She fled Paris just before the Germans occupied it in 1940, returned to New York, and set up the "Art of This Century" Gallery. She donated her collection and the art from her gallery to her uncle's foundation.

Charles V

One of the most influential of European dynasties, the German-Swiss **Hapsburgs** family (also known as Habsburgs) provided rulers for the Holy Roman Empire, and the countries of Spain and Austria.

By the early 16th century, the ruler of the **Holy Roman Empire** was Maximilian I (reigned 1508-1519), a distant relative of the first of the Hapsburg rulers, Rudolf I. Maximilian married Mary of Burgundy and they had a son, Philip I, duke of Burgundy. Philip married Joanna, the daughter of King Ferdinand and Queen Isabella of Spain, and they had two sons.

Their eldest son was **Charles Hapsburg** (reigned 1516–1556) who became Charles I, king of Spain in 1516, and Charles V, Holy Roman Emperor in 1519. As a result of Spain's explorations and conquests, Charles ruled a large empire. It extended from Austria to the Netherlands and across the Atlantic Ocean to Mexico and Peru.

Weary from fighting the Protestants—he resisted Martin Luther and the Reformation—Charles abdicated his throne and retired to a Spanish monastery in 1556, two years before his death. He left Austria and the title of Holy Roman Emperor to his younger brother, **Ferdinand I** (reigned 1558-1564). To his son Philip II, Charles bequeathed Spain, the Netherlands, and the Spanish possessions in the Americas. This split the Austrian and Spanish branches of the Hapsburg family.

Philip II (reigned1556–1598) was a devout Catholic and intended to bring Protestant Europe back to the Roman Catholic Church. He married Mary I, queen of England, but when she died he proposed to her younger sister Elizabeth I, in an attempt to get England to convert back to Catholicism. He failed in this and left England.

Philip sent an enormous fleet of 130 ships called the **Spanish Armada** to invade England in 1588. The Spanish suffered a devastating defeat, and only half their ships returned to Spain.

Philip III (reigned 1598–1621) succeeded his father. During his reign, Spain made peace with England and agreed to a truce with the Netherlands. When his son, Philip IV (reigned 1621-1665), governed Spain, the country came closest to dominating Europe. During the tumultuous Thirty Years' War (1618–48), Philip sent armies throughout Europe, seeking to defeat the English and Dutch and trying to undermine the power of France. When he ultimately failed, Philip was forced to acknowledge the independence of Portugal in 1640 and the Netherlands in 1648.

Charles II (reigned 1665–1700) was the last of the Spanish Hapsburgs. When Charles died, the War of the Spanish Succession erupted in Europe; it ended in 1714 when King Louis XIV of France claimed the throne for his grandson Philip V, duke of Anjou (reigned 1700-1746). This began the line of Spanish Bourbons (see no. 13).

Descendants of European rulers dating back to the 13th century, the Hapsburgs ruled Austria and the Holy Roman Empire—as well as Spain—for hundreds of years.

Ferdinand I (reigned 1558–1564) was the first leader of the Austrian Hapsburgs. The younger brother of King Charles V, he received Austria and the title of **Holy Roman Emperor** when Charles abdicated in 1556. Ferdinand married Anne of Bohemia, and the couple had two sons.

The oldest son, **Maximilian II** (reigned 1527–76), married his first cousin Maria Hapsburg and they had two sons who ruled in the early 17th century. After their deaths, the title passed to their cousin Ferdinand II (reigned 1619-1637). He was followed by his son, Ferdinand III (reigned 1637-1657) who was succeeded by his son, Leopold I (reigned 1658–1705).

Leopold fought for supremacy in Europe with King **Louis XIV** of France. Leopold left the throne to his sons Joseph I (reigned 1705–1711) and Charles VI (reigned 1711–1740). Since Charles had no male heir, he persuaded most of the rulers of Europe to accept the *Pragmatic Sanction*, which called for the right of his daughter, Maria Theresa, to take the throne. When Maria ascended the throne in 1740, most of the great powers quickly broke their word, and the resulting conflict became known as the War of the Austrian Succession (1740–48).

Maria held onto her crown and passed it on to her son, Joseph II (reigned 1780–1790). In 1806 **Napoleon** abolished the Holy Roman Empire, and the Hapsburgs found their realm reduced to only Austria.

The Austrian Hapsburgs then ruled as the "police" of Europe after Napoleon's downfall in 1815, keeping other countries in line with the help of the Austrian army. However, the Hapsburgs were forced to promise a constitu-

Franz Joseph

tion to the Austrian people during the revolution of 1848. The new emperor, **Franz Joseph** (reigned 1848–1916), broke the promise and used force to enter the capital as the absolute monarch once more.

Franz Joseph presided over the last days of grandeur of the Austrian Hapsburgs. He divided his empire into Austria and Hungary and ruled in splendor in **Vienna**. The late 19th century saw Vienna become the world's center for art, music, and medicine.

In 1914, Franz Joseph allowed himself to be drawn into a growing ethnic conflict in the Balkans that led to the assassination of his nephew, Archduke Franz Ferdinand, the heir to the throne. Austria declared war on Serbia, which started a chain of events that led to World War I. Emperor Charles (reigned 1916–18) succeeded Franz Joseph, but abdicated the throne in the last days of the war, thus ending 360 years of Hapsburg rule.

48. Harald-Olaf
Norwegian monarchs

Norway was a land of petty Viking chiefdoms at the start of the ninth century. The chiefdoms became a country due to the actions of a remarkable family of kings, adventurers, fighters—and even a saint.

Harald I (c. A.D. 850–c. 940), often called "Harald Fairhair," succeeded his father, Halfdan the Black, as chief. He came to command a large following, but Harald felt called to greater things. His desire to perform great deeds increased when he sought the hand of Gyda, daughter of Chief Eric. Gyda told Harald that she would marry him only when he had become "king of all **Norway**."

Harald was determined to succeed at the task. He won the Battle of Hafrsfjord in A.D. 872; many of the **Vikings** whom he defeated fled to Iceland. In A.D. 912 he called a convention of chieftains to bestow the royal title on him and his heirs.

Toward the end of his reign, Harald sent his youngest son, **Haakon** (c. A.D. 920–c. 961), to Anglo-Saxon England for his education. Harald abdicated the throne in A.D. 930 in favor of his oldest son, Eric. "Eric Bloodaxe," as he became known, killed seven of his eight brothers before he himself was killed. Haakon (reigned A.D. 934-961), followed Eric, and ruled as the first Christian king of Norway. After Haakon's death, the throne and succession were contested for a number of years. It was not until the reign of **Olaf Tryggvason** that the family reasserted itself.

Olaf Tryggvason (born c. A.D. 968), was a great-grandson of Harald I. He went to England as a Viking marauder in A.D. 994, but returned to Norway as a confirmed Christian. He took the Norwegian throne in A.D. 995 and began to convert his people to Christianity.

Olaf was defeated in a sea battle against the Swedes and Danes in the year 1000. Rather than surrender, he jumped overboard and drowned. After several years of feudal disruptions, Olaf's son **Olaf II** (reigned 1016-1028) succeeded to the throne and continued the work of converting his subjects to Christianity. Olaf II died fighting in the Battle of Stiklestad. He became revered after his death, and was canonized as a saint in 1164. Saint Olaf remains the patron saint of Norway.

After more years of turmoil, Olaf's half brother succeeded to the throne as King **Harald III** (reigned 1046—1066). Harald III returned to the pagan beliefs of his ancestors, and became one of the prominent Viking leaders of his day. He invaded northern England in 1066, but was defeated and killed by the English King Harold Godwinsson.

Norse Sea-King

The Harrisons played vital roles as military and political leaders in building the foundation of the United States.

Benjamin Harrison (c. 1726–1791) , was born in Virginia. He served in the Virginia House of Burgesses before the American Revolution. After 1775, he served in the new Continental Congress, and was one of the signers of the Declaration of Independence.

William Henry Harrison (1773–1841) was a son of Benjamin. In 1791, he entered the U.S. Army, where he served with distinction in campaigns against the Indians. In 1811, Harrison led a force of militia and regulars against the hostile **Shawnees**. Harrison won a decisive victory at the Battle of Tippecanoe, thereby relieving the fears of many frontier Americans. During the War of 1812, he rose to the rank of major general, and won a crucial victory at the Battle of the Thames River in Ontario, Canada, in 1813.

Harrison served in the U.S. House of Representatives from 1816 to 1819 and the U.S. Senate from 1825 to 1828. In 1936, he ran for the presidency as a Whig candidate and lost to Martin Van Buren.

Harrison ran again for president in 1840. This time, he won the election—defeating Van Buren—with 53 percent of the vote and an electoral margin of 234 to 60. However, Harrison caught a severe chill on his inauguration day, March 4, 1841, and died exactly a month later. He was the first American president to die in office.

John Scott Harrison (1809–78) was the second of nine children born to William Henry and Anna Symes. John Scott served in the U.S. House of Representatives from 1853 to 1857. He was the only American ever to be both the son of one president and the father of another.

Benjamin Harrison (1833–1901) was the child of John Scott and Elizabeth Irwin. Benjamin grew up in Ohio and entered the legal profession after college.

Harrison served with distinction during the Civil War, rising to the rank of major general. He then entered politics as a Republican and served in the U.S. Senate from 1881 to 1887. In 1888, he ran for president against Democrat Grover Cleveland. Although he lost the popular vote by about 100,000 votes, Harrison won the election in the electoral college by a vote of 233 to 168.

Harrison's presidency was notable for the passage of the **Sherman Anti-Trust Act**, the Sherman Silver Purchase Act, the McKinley Tariff Act, and the Dependent Pension Act, all passed in 1890. Harrison lost his bid for re-election 1892—running again against Grover Cleveland—and retired from public life.

Benjamin Harrison

50. Hohenzollern Dynasty
Prussian rulers

The foundation for modern German military greatness was actually created by the **Hohenzollern** family, the rulers of Brandenburg-Prussia (modern-day Germany and Poland) centuries before the world wars of the 20th century.

An old aristocratic family that traced its lineage to the 11th century, the Hohenzollerns first achieved prominence in 1417, when **Frederick VI** (1371–1440) received the principality of Brandenburg from the Holy Roman Emperor. This meant that Frederick and his descendants became one of the seven electors to choose the succession of emperors.

In 1525 a minor branch of the family acquired Prussia. Frederick William, "the Great Elector" (1620–1688), integrated the family holdings into a small principality that stretched horizontally across the top of present-day Germany.

The next elector, **Frederick III** (1657–1713), was the first to call himself the king in **Prussia**. This was a rather dubious claim since Germany was full of counts, princes, and dukes, all of whom owed their allegiance to the Holy Roman Emperor, who was usually a Hapsburg.

Frederick William I (1688–1740) concentrated on developing the Prussian army. His son, Frederick II, is usually referred to as **Frederick the Great** (1712–1786). He fought two enormous wars against the combined might of most of Europe and emerged relatively unscathed each time.

Prussia endured dark times during the Napoleonic era. **Napoleon** conquered Prussia and abolished the Holy Roman Empire in 1806. Once Napoleon was defeated and exiled in 1815, Prussia began to emerge as the true leading principality within Germany.

Frederick William III (1770–1840) and Frederick William IV (1795–1861) were con-

Frederick of Hohenzollern

tent to rule Prussia. Wilhelm I (1797–1888), encouraged by the prince-chancellor, **Otto von Bismarck**, began to assert that Prussia was the leader of the true German state. Wilhelm fought three wars against the Danes, Austrians, and French to clear the way of all rivals. His victories overcame the doubts of the other German counts and dukes, and in 1871, he was crowned as king of Prussia and emperor of Germany.

This was the high point for the Hohenzollern family. The following reign of **Wilhelm II** (1859–1941) turned out to be a disaster—and the end of the dynasty. Wilhelm II embraced all of the darkest aspects of Prussian militarism. When the Austrian archduke was assassinated in Sarajevo in August 1914, Wilhelm gave Austria permission to attack Serbia. This led to a declaration of war between Russia and Germany, and the start of World War I. Wilhelm abdicated at the end of World War I, and lived in exile in Holland for the rest of his life.

As scholars, scientists, and writers, the Huxley family achieved the Victorian ideals of higher learning and intellectual inquiry.

The beginnings of the family were quite modest. **T. H. (Thomas Henry) Huxley** (1825–95) was the seventh of eight children born to a schoolteacher in England. He taught himself German and went to medical school in London.

Huxley sailed on the *HMS Rattlesnake* in 1846 and spent most of the next four years onboard the 113-foot frigate, which cruised the Pacific Ocean. Huxley gathered many biological specimens. When he brought his collection back to England, he became an academic superstar at a very early age. He became a professor at the Normal School of Science in 1855. That same year he married Henrietta Ann Heathorn, whom he had first met in Sidney, Australia, while on his cruises. The couple had eight children between 1858 and 1866.

Thomas Huxley

In 1859 naturalist **Charles Darwin** consulted with Huxley before taking the giant step of publishing his revolutionary book *On the Origin of Species* (see no. 28). Once the book was published, Huxley announced that he would be "Darwin's bulldog," defending the controversial theory of evolution. Huxley bested Bishop Samuel Wilberforce in a famous debate over Darwin's theory in 1860. He also wrote *Zoological Evidence as to Man's Place in Nature* (1863).

His son, **Leonard Huxley** (1860–1933),

was both an historian and a private school-master. Acutely conscious of the family's intellectual heritage, Leonard raised his three sons carefully and nurtured their interests.

Julian Huxley (1887–1975), was both a biologist and a philosopher, and taught zoology at the University of London. He was later an administrator for the London Zoo.

Aldous Huxley (1894–1963) was a distinguished novelist, and critic. After graduating from college, Aldous joined the staffs of two literary publications, *Athenaeum* and *Westminster Gazette*. In 1920, he published *Limbo*, a collection of short stories; the following year, he published a successful novel, *Crome Yellow*. His best known work, the dark science-fiction novel *Brave New World*, was published in 1932. A prolific short-story writer and essayist, Aldous continued to publish many works throughout the next few decades. Eventually, he settled in California and became interested in mysticism and Hindu philosophy, views he expressed in his best-seller, *Time Must Have a Stop* (1944). One of his later essays, The *Doors of Perception* (1954), concerned his experimental use of the drug LSD.

Andrew Fielding Huxley (b. 1917) became a noted physiologist. He shared the 1963 Nobel Prize for medicine with two collaborators for their work in the analysis of nerve impulses and their conduction. He received a knighthood in 1974.

At the turn of the 20th century, the James family stood out as a shining example of the growing sophistication of American intellectual thought. The family's prominence began when **Henry James, Sr.** (1811–82) saw to the careful, and some might say obsessive, schooling of his children.

Henry was born in Albany, New York, the son of a very wealthy merchant. After the death of his father, Henry had enough money to pursue a life of educated leisure. He married Mary Robertson Walsh in 1840, and the couple had five children.

Henry's son, **William James** (1842–1910) was born in New York City. After being taught by private tutors and traveling through Europe with the entire James family, he earned his M.D. at Harvard in 1869. William then fell into a serious depression, from which he emerged with a new belief in the importance of free will. Beginning in 1885, he taught philosophy and psychology for more than 20 years at Harvard.

William wrote many books, the most significant of which were *The Principles of Psychology* (1890), *The Varieties of Religious Experience* (1902), and *Pragmatism* (1907). In these works, he probed the meaning of neurosis, self-doubt, and the need for a transcendent philosophy. At the time of his death, he was recognized as the foremost philosopher in the United States.

Henry's son **Henry James, Jr.** (1843–1916) was also born in New York City. Like his older brother, he received a vigorous training in the classics at home. He went to Harvard and then **Harvard Law School**. He eventually settled in England in 1883, and did not return to the United States for 20 years.

For 40 years, Henry was one of the most well-known popular novelists of his day. His experiences in both America and Europe gave

him material for his early works: *Roderick Hudson* (1876), *The American* (1877), *The Europeans* (1878), and the story that made him famous, *Daisy Miller* (1879). Some of his later works, such as *The Portrait of a Lady* (1881), and *The Bostonians* (1886), were less successful, and he turned to writing plays in

William James

the early 1890s. This move proved to be a critical and commercial failure, and he returned to writing novels. He then produced some of his most successful works including, the stories *The Turn of the Screw* (1898) and *The Awkward Age* (1899), and the novels *The Wings of the Dove* (1902), *The Ambassadors* (1903), and *The Golden Bowl* (1904).

Through the careers of William and his brother Henry, the James family set a standard for intellectual brilliance that has seldom been equaled in American life.

Perhaps no family in the history of the American West can boast of its importance in its time as much as the Johnson and Brant family of upstate New York.

William Johnson (1714–74) was born in Smithtown, near Dublin, Ireland. He emigrated to the New York colony in 1737 and managed the estates of his uncle, a British sea captain named Peter Warren. These lands were located in the Mohawk River Valley, which was a gateway through the Appalachian Mountains to Lake Ontario. It was also the home of the tribes of the six Iroquois Nations: the Mohawk, Oneida, Onondaga, Seneca, Cayuga, and Tuscarora.

William Johnson

Johnson married a German woman, **Catherine Weisenberg**, and the couple had three children. By mid-century, Johnson had left his uncle's service and had become the foremost landowner in the Mohawk Valley. Ever mindful of the importance of the Native Americans, he befriended the Mohawks. Johnson was invited to their councils and became uniquely skilled at diplomacy in both the colonial and Native American worlds.

When the **French and Indian War** began in 1755, Johnson raised a combined force of settlers and Mohawks and tried to capture the French fort, St. Frederic, near the head of Lake Champlain. He failed in that effort, but he did win an important victory at the Battle of Lake George.

Catherine died in 1759, and later that year Johnson married an Iroquois woman named **Mary Brant** (c. 1736–1796). Mary became renowned for her oratorical skills and her ability to persuade the chiefs to follow her lead. Mary's younger brother **Joseph Brant** (1742–1807) also benefited from his alliance to her husband and became one of the leading Mohawk chiefs.

Johnson died in 1774, just before the start of the **American Revolution.** When the war began, his son and heir by Catherine Weisenberg, Sir John Johnson (1742–1830), attempted to remain neutral. Failing in that, he declared himself a **Loyalist** and fled to British Canada. Sir John and his cousin Guy Johnson, William's nephew, led border raids against New York settlements during the war.

Joseph Brant went to London in 1775. After being treated as a celebrity by London society, he returned to Canada and led his Mohawk warriors in bloody raids along the Mohawk River Valley frontier. When the war turned against the British and their Native American allies, many **Iroquois** suffered greatly. American troops marched through their villages, destroying the buildings and burning the crops.

After the war, Joseph and Mary Brant settled in present-day Ontario, Canada. They lived a life of dignified exile there and remained important Native American leaders.

54. Kamehameha
Hawaiian rulers

The Kamehameha family ruled the Hawaiian Islands for four generations. The family leaders performed a balancing act, flirting with American and European powers, and keeping their own sovereignty.

Kamehameha I (c. 1737–1819), originally called Paiea, was the son of an important Hawaiian chief. In 1782 the islands were divided between Paiea and his cousin, Kiwalaotk. The cousins fought a brief war against each other later that year. Kiwalaotk was killed and Kamehameha began to bring all the islands of **Hawaii** under his rule. It took until 1810 to accomplish this.

Kamehameha was a vigorous, enlightened king. He outlawed human sacrifice, set up territorial governors on each of the islands, and instituted the Kanawai or "law of the splintered paddle," which protected Hawaiians from the authority of their local chiefs. He created a government monopoly in the sandalwood trade, and imposed port duties on European ships that visited the islands.

Kamehameha's son **Liholiho** (1797-1824) ascended the throne after his father's death. As King Kamehameha II (reigned 1819–1824), he allowed the first Christian missionaries into Hawaii. When he and two of his wives went on a state visit to England in 1823, he and one of the wives contracted measles and died in London.

Kauikeaouli the younger brother of Liholiho, became King **Kamehameha III** (reigned 1814–1854) when he was only 10 years old; a princess regent was appointed to rule in his youth. Once he truly became king, Kamehameha III was a progressive monarch. He enacted important laws, such as the Declaration of Right (1839) and the Edict of Toleration (1839), and wrote the first constitution for Hawaii that favored a constitutional monarchy. Kamehameha III obtained formal recognition of his country's sovereignty

from the United States in 1842 and Great Britain and France in 1843.

Kamehameha IV (reigned 1855-1863), was a nephew and adopted son of Kamehameha III. He vigorously opposed efforts to make Hawaii part of the United States. Oddly enough, he sold the Hawaiian island of Niihau to a Scotswoman, Mrs. Elizabeth Sinclair, in 1864.

Lot, who became **Kamehameha V** (reigned1863–1872), was the older brother of Kamehameha IV. He wrote a new constitution for Hawaii in 1864 and was the first member of his family to import Japanese laborers. Kamehameha V never married and left no heirs; after his death, the Hawaiian legislature elected his cousin William Charles to be the new king.

The Kamehameha monarchy ended when American investors in the sugar industry wrested economic and political control from **Queen Liliuokalani** (reigned 1891–1893). A new provisional government proclaimed Hawaii an American protectorate on February 1, 1893.

Kamehameha I

61

The **Kano** family emerged during the 15th century as Japanese artists who adapted and expanded certain painting techniques borrowed from the Chinese. By the 17th century, the Kanos were the official court painters of the **Tokugawa** shoguns, the military commanders who ruled Japan.

Kano Kagenobu (c. 1400–c. 1450) was a samurai, descended from a long line of warriors. He became an amateur painter, and historians believe that in 1432 he made a painting of Mount Fuji for a visit by the shogun Achikaga Yoshinori.

Kagenobu's son, **Kano Masanobu** (1434–1530), trained to be a painter in the kanga painting style of Chinese ink. He concentrated on Buddhist themes and depictions of nature. *Bamboo* and *White Crane and Chinese Moutain Landscape* are among his best-known works that have survived throughout the centuries.

It was Masanobu's son, **Kano Motonobu** (1476–1559), who created a synthesis between the Chinese kanga style and the lovely colors of the Japanese yamato-e style. Among Motonobu's best-known works are *Flowers and Birds* and *Four Accomplishments*. The latter refers to the accomplishments of Japanese gentlemen: calligraphy, painting, lute playing, and the game of go.

Kano Eitoku (1543–1590),was a grandson of Motonobu. He became the leading painter of the *Momoyama* period during the last quarter of the 16th century in Japan. Eitoku enjoyed the favor and patronage of Japanese shogun **Oda Nobunaga**. In 1576, Eitoku created enormous wall paintings to decorate Nobunaga's Azuchi Castle. The artwork was used to glorify the dynamism of Nobunaga's rule and to intimidate his subjects. Eitoku's son, Kano Takanobu, died at any early age and leadership of the family school passed to three of Eitoku's grandsons.

Kano Tanyu (1602–1647) became the leader of a new branch of the school, established in the city of Edo (Tokyo) after it became the capital of Japan in 1615. Tanyu became court painter to the Tokugawa shogun and he painted the walls of Nijo Castle in Kyoto. Along with his grandfather, Eitoku, and his great great-grandfather, Motonobu, he is remembered as one of the "three famous brushes" of the family school.

Tanyu's brother, **Kano Naonobu** (1607–1650) was known for his "grass" style of brushwork, which used broad, uninhibited strokes and an ink wash. Their brother, Kano Yasunobu (1613–1685), collaborated in the decoration of the shogun mausoleum at Nikko.

Although later members of the Kano family were less renowned than the first seven generations, the family remained the official court painters for nearly another 200 years, until the end of the shogunate in 1868.

Oda Nobunaga

Joseph P. Kennedy & family

Perhaps the most celebrated American family of the 20th century is the Kennedys of Massachusetts.

The patriarch of the Kennedy clan was **Joseph P. Kennedy** (1886–1969). In 1914, he married Rose Fitzgerald (1890–1995) and they raised a large family in Boston, New York City, and Hyannisport on Cape Cod.

Kennedy had large political ambitions for his sons. The family pinned their hopes on **John Fitzgerald Kennedy** (1917–63) when their intended political star, son Joe, Jr., was killed while on a bombing raid during World War II.

John Kennedy entered politics in 1946 as a representative from **Massachusetts**; in 1952 he was elected to the U.S. Senate. In 1960, he ran for president and defeated Richard Nixon in the closest popular vote in history. Kennedy appointed his younger brother Robert Francis (1923–1968) to serve as U.S. attorney general during his administration. Their youngest brother, Edward Kennedy (b. 1923), became a U.S. senator in 1962.

With the growing civil rights movement, the creation of the Peace Corps, and the space race, Kennedy's presidency was a time of great political interest and personal hope for many Americans. The president's charm and the sophistication of his wife, first lady **Jacqueline Bouvier** (1929-1994) , won the hearts of millions of Americans. Then suddenly the glamour and excitement of Kennedy's presidency ended in tragedy when Lee Harvey Oswald assassinated the president in Dallas in 1963.

Robert Kennedy represented New York in the U.S. Senate from 1964 to 1968. He was considered the front-runner for the 1968 Democratic presidential nomination after winning the California primary on June 6. However, that night he was shot and killed in a Los Angeles hotel by Sirhan Sirhan.

Edward Kennedy's political career was damaged in 1969 by his involvement in the drowning death of a woman passenger in a car he was driving. In 1980, he made an attempt to unseat President **Jimmy Carter** for the Democratic presidential nomination, but failed. He then chose to remain in the U.S. Senate, and continued to serve with distinction there for the next two decades.

The third generation of Kennedys continued the family's involvement in politics and public service throughout the rest of the 20th century. Joseph P. Kennedy II (b. 1952) represented Massachusetts in Congress from 1986-1998. Patrick J. Kennedy (b. 1967) was elected to congress from Rhode Island in 1994. Kathleen Kennedy Townsend (b. 1951) became Lieutenant Governor of Maryland in 1995.

J.F.K.'s son, John F. Kennedy, Jr. (1960-1999), became the founder and publisher of the political magazine, *George*, in 1995. Tragically, like his father, John, Jr. also met an early death; he was killed, along with his wife and sister-in-law, in a private plane crash off the Massachusetts coast in July 1999.

57. Krupp
German industrialists

Perhaps the wealthiest and most prestigious family of arms merchants in history was the Krupp family of Germany.

Already a member of a successful merchant family, Friederich Krupp (1787–1826) started a steel-casting plant in 1811 in Essen, in the Ruhr River Valley. When he died, his 14-year-old son, **Alfred Krupp** (1812–87), took over leadership of the company. Alfred began with seven workers, but by the time of his death, the Krupp family employed more than 21,000 people. Alfred experimented with toolmaking, and manufactured the first seamless steel railway tire in 1852. He also brought the sophisticated Bessemer steelmaking process to Germany, and began making steel cannons in the 1850s. These weapons were instrumental in Germany's victory in the Franco-Prussian War.

Alfred's son, **Friederich Alfred Krupp** (1854–1902), ran the company after his father's death. The firm continued to expand as it supplied the German empire with weaponry, and in 1902, Friederich acquired the massive shipbuilding yards at Kiel, in northern Germany. He died that same year and was succeeded by his daughter, **Bertha Krupp** (1886–1957).

Bertha married Gustav von Bohlen und Halbach (1870–1950), and the couple jointly ran the company. During **World War I**, their "Big Bertha" howitzers (42-centimeter siege mortars) were a striking symbol of the Krupp's importance to the German war machine. Germany lost the war, however, and the Krupps were forced to switch to manufacturing agricultural tools when the fighting ended.

Bertha and Gustav's son, Alfried Krupp von Bohlen und Halbach (1907–67), joined Hitler's "Blackshirts" in 1931; his father decided to support the Nazis a year later. Under Hitler's leadership, Germany began to

Friederich Krupp II

rearm during the 1930s. Since this was illegal under the **Treaty of Versailles**, the Krupps disguised their tank-building activities as an "agricultural tractor program."

After World War II ended with Germany's defeat, the family was investigated by the Allied war crimes tribunal at **Nuremberg**. Bertha and Gustav were judged to be too old to stand trial. Alfried was convicted of war crimes for using slave labor during the war. He was sentenced to 12 years in prison, and the firm and family fortune were confiscated.

Surprisingly, Alfried's sentence was commuted by a U.S. judge in 1951, and his property was restored. After promising never again to create weapons, he re-energized the firm and began producing steel to rebuild war-torn Europe. By the early 1960s, Alfried employed more than 125,000 workers and was himself worth more than $1 billion. When Alfried died in 1967, the running of the company was turned over to business people outside the immediate family.

Native American history is filled with tales of prominent families, and the La Flesches of the Plains tribes were among the most influential.

Joseph La Flesche (1822–c. 1882) — known as "Iron Eye"—was the son of a French fur trader and a Native American woman from the Omaha tribe. He met **Mary Gale**, who was part Iowa and part Omaha, and the two married in 1843. Although he had two other wives, all eight of his children were raised as full brothers and sisters, not as half-siblings.

La Flesche believed that Native Americans needed to conform to the white man's ways to survive. He converted to **Presbyterianism** and raised his children in a manner that allowed them to function as members of either culture.

Susette La Flesche (1854–1903), also known as "Bright Eyes," was born at her father's home near Bellevue, Nebraska. She studied both on the reservation and in white schools. She then returned to the Omaha Reservation and taught in a government school.

In 1879 Susette was deeply moved by the plight of 35 **Ponca**s who had made a 600-mile journey to the Omaha Reservation. The Poncas were arrested and ordered back to the Indian Territory in present-day Oklahoma. Thomas Tibbles, a reporter for the *Omaha Herald*, enlisted two lawyers to speak for the Poncas. After the Poncas were freed in April, 1879, Susette, Tibbles, and the Ponca leader

Susette La Flesche

Standing Bear toured the eastern United States together, speaking out for Native American rights.

Susette married Tibbles in 1881; the couple lived in Lincoln, Nebraska. After Susette's death in 1903, Tibbles ran for vice president on the People's (Populist) Party ticket, but lost the race.

Susette's brother, **Francis La Flesche** (1857–1932), was born on the Omaha Reservation. He became an anthropologist and an adviser for the Bureau of Indian Affairs around 1881. He and Alice Cunningham Fletcher co-authored *A Study of Omaha Music* (1893) *and The Omaha Tribe* (1911).

Susan La Flesche (1865–1915), the daughter of Joseph La Flesche and Mary Gale, studied with Christian missionaries as a child and then attended the Hampton Institute in Virginia. She graduated first in her class of 36 students from the **Women's Medical College** of Pennsylvania in 1889. She was the first Native American to receive a degree in medicine.

Susan married Henry Picotte, who was one-half Sioux and one-half French. She developed a private practice in Bancroft, Nebraska. During a 25-year period, she treated almost all of the 1,300 members of the Omaha tribe, who were scattered across the reservation.

The House of Lancaster occupied the English throne during the 15th century, but began its rise to prominence and power two hundred years before.

Edmund of Lancaster (1245–96) became the first earl of Lancaster, a city on the northwest coast of England. He was the second son of King Henry III and Eleanor of Provence. He fought in a crusade and against the Welsh, then died while leading an army in France.

Thomas of Lancaster (1278–1322), Edmund's son, led the English barons in their opposition to his cousin, King Edward II of England. As a consequence, Thomas fell from power and was executed for treason. His brother, Henry of Lancaster (c.1290-1345),

Death of Richard III

continued the family tradition of leading the English barons in rebellion against the king. Henry captured King Edward II in 1324 and was commander of the castle in which the monarch was subsequently held prisoner.

Henry of Grossmont (c. 1300–1361), the fourth earl of Lancaster, was named duke of Lancaster in 1351. He led English forces against both the Scots and the Moors. Henry died without a male heir and the title went to his son-in-law, John of Gaunt (1340–1399).

The fourth son of King Edward III, John of Gaunt was renowned for his success as both a soldier and an ambassador. John held the title of duke of Lancaster, while his brother, Edmund, was made the first duke of York. Edmund's descendants established the House of York, which would become the great enemy of the House of Lancaster.

Henry of Bolingbroke (1366–1413) was the son and heir of John of Gaunt. He became King Henry IV of England (reigned 1399-1413), thereby starting the Lancastrian monarchy. His son, Henry V (reigned 1413–1422), won a crushing victory over the French at Agincourt in 1415.

Henry VI (reigned 1422–1461) was a weak king, steered by his advisers and thwarted by the English barons who opposed his rule. It was during his lifetime that the **Wars of the Roses** began. The House of Lancaster and the House of York fought against each other for more than 30 years, each family seeking to gain and hold the kingdom.

In 1483, **Richard III**, from the House of York, laid claim to the throne. His rule lasted only two years; he was killed by Duke Henry of Richmond at the **Battle of Bosworth Field** in 1485. The Wars of the Roses ended, and Henry took the throne as the first ruler of the House of Tudor, King Henry VII (reigned 1485–1509).

60. Leakey
English scientists

Where did the human species first come from? This is the central question that has burned in the minds of the **Leakey** family of scientists.

When **Louis Seymour Bazett Leakey** (1903–72) was born, most scientists believed that the origins of humankind lay in Asia. However, Louis and his family proved that humans first evolved in Africa.

Leakey was born in Kabete, Kenya, the son of British missionaries. His father, Canon Harry Leakey, translated the Bible into the African language *Kikuyu*.

Louis was initiated into the local tribe before he went to England to study at Cambridge University. He graduated with honors in 1926, and went immediately to east Africa for the first of the four expeditions he made between 1926 and 1935. Louis made his first trip to Olduvai Gorge in the Serengeti Plain during 1931 and 1932. Louis's studies there confirmed his belief that humankind had first evolved in **Africa**; however, he had further research to complete before he could persuade his fellow scientists.

Mary Douglas Nicol (1913–1996) was born in London. Her father was a painter, and she became an expert at drawing stone artifacts after studying archaeology in France. Her drawings brought her into contact with Louis. They married in 1936 and had three children.

They moved to **Kenya** in 1937 and began to concentrate their studies in the Olduvai Gorge area. On July 17, 1959, Mary found the remains of a prehuman cranium, which were later dated at around 1.75 million years old. In 1960 Mary established a permanent base camp at the Olduvai Gorge. That year the Leakeys found the first fossils of *Homo habilis*, a human ancestor.

Louis became curator of Kenya's Coryndon Memorial Museum. Mary carried on their work, and in 1974 she discovered the remains of *australopithecine*—a small-brained, large-toothed, apelike human ancestor—which showed that prehumans walked upright at an early age. She found the first set of *hominid,* (upright primate), footprints in 1976.

The working relationship of husband and wife endured for more than 30 years. As Louis aged, Mary increasingly became the leader of the partnership.

Louis and Mary's son, **Richard Leakey** (b. 1944), learned his scientific skills while working with his parents. In 1974 he became director of the National Museums of Kenya. He found the skull of a two-million-year-old *Australopithecus boisei* in 1972. He is also well known for his organization of wildlife conservation groups.

The Leakeys in London, 1950

67

For nearly 100 years, the Lee family produced many of the renowned leaders in American politics and military history.

The Lee family established their estate, Stratford, in Westmoreland County, Virginia. Four Lee brothers left that estate to lead the colonial fight during the American Revolution.

The oldest of the brothers, **Richard Henry Lee** (1732–1794), was a politician. He presented the resolution of the Virginia Convention to the Continental Congress on June 7, 1776, that the 13 colonies should be free and independent of Great Britain.

Richard's brothers also made important contributions during the war. **Francis Lightfoot Lee** (1734–1797) was one of the signers of the Declaration of Independence. William Lee (1739–1795) negotiated a treaty between the new United States and the United Provinces of the Netherlands in 1780. Arthur Lee (1740–1792) was one of three American commissioners sent to France in 1776, and he signed the colonies' treaty with France in 1778.

A cousin of the Lees of Stratford, Henry Lee (1756–1818), emerged as a capable and daring cavalry commander during the **Revolutionary War**. Lee led his green-jacketed troops to victory on a number of occasions and was present at the final American victory at Yorktown.

Robert Edward Lee (1807–1770) was a son of Henry Lee. He graduated second in his class from West Point Military Academy in 1829. Lee first rose to prominence during the Mexican War, where he distinguished himself in brilliant scouting maneuvers. When the **Civil War** began in 1861, Lee was offered the overall command of the Union armies.

Torn between his allegiance to the United States and his love for the state of Virginia, Lee chose the latter. He entered the **Confederate** service in 1861, and by 1862 he was commander of the Army of Northern Virginia, the major fighting force of the Confederacy. Lee led his soldiers to brilliant victories at Fredericksburg and Chancellorsville. However, each time he invaded the North, Lee met disaster. He was defeated at Antietam in 1862 and at **Gettysburg** in 1863. From then on, he was permanently on the defensive.

In the last phase of the war, Lee fought Union general **Ulysses S. Grant** in a grueling set of battles in and around Richmond. Lee and his army escaped from the siege of Richmond, but Grant pursued him, and Lee chose to surrender his sword at Appomattox Court House on April 9, 1865, thus ending the Civil War. Lee then became a private citizen and served as president of Washington College in Virginia until his death.

Robert E. Lee

The Le Moynes of Montreal became the most distinguished family of settlers, fighters, and explorers in French North America.

Charles Le Moyne (1626–83) was born in Dieppe, Normandy (in modern-day France). He went to the **Quebec** colony in Canada in 1641 as a contracted employee of the Jesuit fathers. After learning a number of Native American languages, including **Iroquois**, Le Moyne settled in Montreal. He served with distinction in the French wars against the Iroquois, and often served as an interpreter between the two sides.

Le Moyne married **Catherine Tierry** in 1654. The couple had 12 sons and 2 daughters, nearly all of whom figured prominently in the history of New France.

Charles Le Moyne de Longueuil (1656–1729), the oldest child, served bravely in battles against the Iroquois; like his father, he was an interpreter and negotiator. King Louis XIV made him a baron in 1700; he was the only French Canadian so honored.

Pierre Le Moyne d'Iberville (1661–1706) was the most famous member of the family. He raided English trading posts on Hudson Bay and later ravaged English settlements in Newfoundland and present-day Maine. Then he moved his activities to the south and made the first successful French navigation of the

Pierre Le Moyne d'Iberville

Mississippi Delta from the Gulf of Mexico. King Louis XIV knighted him for his accomplishments. In 1706, Iberville returned to the Caribbean and died of fever after an attack on English Jamaica.

Paul Le Moyne de Maricourt (1663–1704) served as an interpreter and diplomat in the French wars against the Iroquois. Joseph Le Moyne de Serigny et de Loire (1688–1734) became a naval officer in the service of King Louis XIV, and during the 1720s, he governed the important naval base of Rochefort, France.

Jean Baptiste Le Moyne de Bienville (1680–1767) , the youngest of the 12 sons, accompanied Pierre on a reconnaissance of the Mississippi River in 1699. Jean Baptiste later returned to Louisiana on his own and was among the settlers who laid out the town of New Orleans in 1718. Later he served as governor of the province of Louisiana. He went to France after the Treaty of Paris ceded the colony to Spain in 1763.

Explorers, merchants, linguists, diplomats, and nobles, the sons of the Le Moyne family served the interests of the **Bourbon** monarchy, the colonies of New France and Louisiana, and their own ambitions, to make a lasting impact on 17th and 18th century life in the New World.

Members of the Loge and Cabot families have provided distinguished public service for their country since the founding days of the republic.

George Cabot (1752–1823) was born in Salem, Massachusetts. He became a merchant and built privateers—armed ships that seized British merchant vessels and kept the cargo—during the American Revolution. Cabot became the first U.S. senator from Massachusetts. Under his leadership, the U.S. Senate approved the controversial Jay Treaty in 1795 in an effort to improve American-British relations.

Cabot's granddaughter, Anna Cabot, married John Lodge of Boston. Their first son was **Henry Cabot Lodge** (1850–1924). He graduated from Harvard, earned both a law degree and a Ph.D. in political science, and then entered politics as a Republican. Lodge served in the U.S. House of Representatives from 1887 to 1893, and then became a U.S. senator for the rest of his life.

Lodge supported America's entry into World War I. However, he strongly opposed President Woodrow Wilson's plan for a **League of Nations** following the end of the war. Lodge insisted that the United States not bind itself to acting in concert with other nations. As a result Lodge—and the powerful Republican Senate leadership—persuaded their colleagues to reject the Treaty of Versailles, and the United States did not join the League.

Henry Cabot Lodge, Jr. (1902–85) was born in Nahant, Massachusetts, and worked as a reporter before entering politics. He served in the U.S. Senate from 1937 to 1944 and then resigned to go on active duty overseas. He rose to the rank of lieutenant colonel during World War II, and then returned to the U.S. Senate where he served from 1947 to 1953. Lodge was defeated for re-election in

Henry Cabot Lodge

1952 by political newcomer John F. Kennedy.

He then served as U.S. representative to the **United Nations** from 1953–60. That year he ran for vice president on the Republican ticket with Richard Nixon; they were defeated by John Kennedy and Lyndon Johnson. Loge finished his career by serving twice as U.S. ambassador to the Republic of South Vietnam (1963–64 and 1965–67).

John Davis Lodge (1903–85), a younger brother of Henry, Jr., graduated from Harvard, and then Harvard Law School. He served in Congress from 1947 to 1951, then as governor of Connecticut from 1951 to 1955. Lodge later had a long diplomatic career, serving as ambassador to Spain (1955–61), Argentina (1969–74), and Switzerland (1983).

The contributions of the remarkable Lowell family can be seen in the fields of politics, arts, science, and industry in the United States.

John Lowell (1743–1802),was the descendant of a merchant family that emigrated to the Massachusetts Bay Colony in 1639. He served in the Continental Congress and became a distinguished judge. John's son, John Lowell II (1769–1840), was noted for his opposition to the War of 1812. He believed that the British were justified in their use of impressment—the practice of taking sailors off American ships and "pressing" them into British naval service.

Francis Cabot Lowell (1775–1817) was born in Newburyport, Massachusetts. He graduated from Harvard College and entered the merchant trade. In 1812 he formed the Boston Manufacturing Company. Lowell led the building of the Waltham Factory, which was the first in the world to combine all the stages of cotton manufacturing under one roof. Nine years after his death, a new textile town was named Lowell in his honor.

Three of John Lowell II's great-grandchildren became prominent in the arts and sciences. Percival Lowell (1855–1916) graduated from Harvard in 1876 and then studied astronomy. In 1894 he set up the **Lowell Observatory** in Flagstaff, Arizona, where he studied the stars with an 18-inch refracting telescope. In 1907, Percival took the first good photographs of Mars.

His brother Abbott Lawrence Lowell (1856–1943) became a professor of government at Harvard University, and served as its president from 1909 until 1933.

Their sister, **Amy Lowell** (1874–1925), became an earnest advocate of the new school of *imagism* founded by poet Ezra Pound, which stressed concentration, clear images, new rhythms, and use of common speech. Amy's first major work was *Sword Blades and*

Poppy Seeds (1914). She posthumously won the 1926 Pulitzer Prize, awarded, for her collection of verse, *What's O'Clock* (1925).

James Russell Lowell (1819–1891), a cousin of the Lowell siblings, was a poet, dramatist, essayist, and diplomat. He gained recognition for his work in the arts and his anti-slavery writing during the 1840s. He was the first editor of *Atlantic Monthly* magazine

Percival Lowell

and later served as minister to Spain (1877–80) and England (1880–85).

Robert Lowell, Jr. (1917–1977), great-grandnephew of James Russell, was born in Boston and graduated from Kenyon College. He served one year in prison for his stance as a conscientious objector during World War II. He wrote on governmental and societal themes, and is perhaps best known for his play *The Old Glory* published in 1965. Robert's *Lord Weary's Castle* won a Pulitzer Prize for poetry in 1947.

American Puritans believed that the family unit was the best possible vessel of God's mission on earth. Many of the early Massachusetts Puritans had large families. One of the most significant of these was the Mather family.

Richard Mather (1596–1669) was born in Lowton, Lancashire, England. He married Katherine Holt in 1624, and the couple emi-

Cotton Mather

grated to the Massachusetts Bay Colony in 1635. As a minister in Dorchester, Massachusetts, Mather soon became known as one of the most forceful defenders of the Puritan faith.

His son, **Increase Mather** (1638–1723), was born in Dorchester. He graduated from Harvard College and went to England in the late 1650s. There, he witnessed the change of government from Oliver Cromwell's Puritan regime to the restored monarchy of King **Charles II**. Upset by this development,

Mather went home to Massachusetts. He married Maria Cotton in 1662 and became minister of the Second Church of Boston that year.

Mather returned to England in the late 1680s. His mission was to persuade King James II to restore the Massachusetts Bay Charter, a document that had guaranteed the rights of the Puritans to govern themselves. He failed in this attempt. After King James II was overthrown in the **Glorious Revolution** of 1688, Mather managed to persuade King William III to grant a new charter to Massachusetts. Mather returned to his home colony with the new charter in 1692.

During his father's absence, Increase's son, **Cotton Mather** (1663–1728), had become a prominent Massachusetts leader in his own right. Ordained as a minister in 1685, he preached at the Second Church of Boston in his father's absence. Cotton was an extremely prolific author and wrote nearly 450 books and pamphlets during his lifetime.

The **Salem** Witch Trials of 1692 presented a crisis to the Mather family. While Increase remained quiet about the issue, Cotton took a moderate stand toward the situation. He announced his belief that fasting and prayer were better remedies that punitive legal actions. However, when 19 "witches" were hanged, Mather wrote pamphlets defending the action of the judges. The controversy that resulted from the trials served to lessen the power of the Mathers. Although they remained influential within the church, they had less authority in public matters after the trials were over.

Cotton's son **Samuel Mather** (1706-1785) preached at Boston's Second Congregational Church for 19 years. In 1741, he was dismissed by his congregation, but 93 members of his congregation left with him. They founded a new church where he preached for many years.

During the late third century B.C., the Maurya family of Indian rulers was renowned for its peculiar combination of ferocity and gentleness, barbarity and kindness.

Chandragupta Maurya (reigned c. 321–c. 297 B.C.) overthrew the ruler of the Indian kingdom of Magadh, a nation as large as France, based in the central Ganges Valley. He accomplished this because India's kingdoms were in disarray after the invasion of Alexander the Great. Chandragupta seized the throne around 321 B.C. and began to build a power base in northeastern India.

In 305 B.C., Chandragupta was challenged by Seleucus Nicator, one of Alexander's former generals, then the governor of **Babylon**. Chandragupta successfully defended his kingdom, and Seleucus agreed to leave India alone. From that time forward, Chandragupta was able to run his kingdom independently.

He built a magnificent capital at Pataliputra (present-day Patna), near the confluence of the Son and Ganges rivers. He also created a strong bureaucracy that enforced his decrees.

It is believed, though not certain, that Chandragupta embraced the **Jainist** faith of self-denial and nonviolence in his later years and that he abdicated the throne to become a monk.

Bindusara (reigned 298–273 B.C.), a son of Chandragupta, inherited the throne. Very little is known of his life and rule, and historical records are vague until Bindusara's son, Asoka, came to power.

Asoka (reigned 273–238 B.C.) began his rule as a conqueror in the family tradition. He made war on the kingdom of Kalinga to the southwest, killed 100,000 of its people, and took 150,000 prisoners. Then he underwent a personal transformation. Horrified by what he had seen of war, Asoka became a Buddhist. He adopted the practice of *ahimsa*, or non-injury to all living beings.

To honor his new beliefs, Asoka abstained from eating meat. He had hospitals built, wells dug, and sponsored the building of temples throughout his empire. He wrote a number of edicts that were inscribed on stone pillars, 30 of which are still in existence. In everything he did, Asoka urged mindfulness and compassion for all living beings.

India's emblem carved for Asoka

Asoka also sent **Buddhist** missionaries to other Asian countries, seeking to convert the peoples of the world. His son Mahinda is said to have been responsible for the conversion of the people of the island of Ceylon (present-day Sri Lanka).

Asoka died in 238 B.C. The descendants of Chandragupta and Asoka were far less capable than these two great leaders, and the empire fell apart within 50 years of Asoka's death.

The Mayos are one of the great families of American medicine; their contributions continue through the services of Mayo clinics in Minnesota, Arizona, and Florida.

William Worrall Mayo (1819–1911) was born in Manchester, England. He attended Owens College in Manchester before emigrating to the United States in 1845. Mayo earned his M.D. at the University of Missouri in 1855, and by 1863 he had settled in Rochester, Minnesota. There he built a respected surgical practice. He served as an army surgeon during the Great Sioux Uprising in 1862. Then in 1889, with the help of his sons and the nuns of a local convent, he built St. Mary's Hospital in **Rochester.**

His son, William James Mayo (1861–1939), was born in LaSueur, Minnesota. He earned his M.D. at the University of Michigan in 1883, and in 1889 he joined his father on the staff of the Sisters of St. Francis's St. Mary's Hospital. William James specialized in stomach and gall bladder surgery. He traveled widely to educate himself in new surgical techniques, and he served in the U.S. Army Medical Corps during World War I.

Charles Horace Mayo (1865–1939) was the younger brother of William James. Born in Rochester, he earned his M.D. at the Chicago Medical College in 1888. Showing a special talent for surgery, he specialized in treatments of the thyroid gland. Later he expanded his specialties to include treatment of the nervous system and eye surgeries.

The brothers, William James and Charles Horace, founded the **Mayo Clinic** in 1903 as an outgrowth of the work they had both done at St. Mary's Hospital. Although William acted as the clinic's administrator, both brothers made all the decisions. The brothers performed all the surgery at the clinic until 1905; then the clinic began to expand and other doctors were hired. The Mayo brothers gave $1.5 million to the University of Minnesota in 1915, thereby creating the Mayo Foundation for Medical Education and Research.

Charles William Mayo (1898-1968) was the son of Charles Horace Mayo. He earned his M.D. at the University of Pennsylvania in 1926 and became a surgeon at the Mayo Clinic in 1931. He remained there until his retirement in 1963, specializing in intestinal surgery.

William W. Mayo

68. Médici
Italian bankers, politicians, and religious leaders

The name Médici is almost synonymous with the Italian Renaissance—and conjures up images of wealth, power, and artistic patronage. The Médici first lived several miles north of Florence, Italy, but sometime during the early 13th century, they moved into the city.

The **Médici** family first obtained wealth and prominence as merchants. A Médici son, Giovanni di Bicci (1360–1429), became general manager of a bank in Rome and was given the lucrative position of banker to the pope. His two sons, Cosimo and Lorenzo, founded the "older" and "younger" branches of the family, and began the long tradition of patronage of the arts and learning.

Cosimo de Médici (1389–1464) was an extremely capable banker and political leader, although he always exerted his influence behind the scenes.

His grandson, **Lorenzo de Médici** (1449–1492), "Lorenzo the Magnificent," became the next powerful member of the family. Lorenzo directed both the internal and foreign affairs of Florence. He sponsored Michelangelo, who created magnificent artworks that glorified **Florence** and the Médici. Lorenzo ruled the city informally, in the manner of his grandfather.

Piero de Médici (1472–1503) was less capable than his father. When his politics contributed to a French invasion of Italy in 1494, Piero fled the city and leadership passed to Giuliano de Médici (1475–1516). Just as it seemed the family influence was waning, two Médici family members came forward to take Christianity's highest post, the papacy itself. Giovanni de Médici (1475-1521), one of Lorenzo the Magnificent's three sons, became Pope **Leo X** in 1513.

Pope Leo X and later Pope Clement VII, who was Giulio de Médici (1478–1554), the illegitimate son of Lorenzo's younger brother, presided over the church just as Martin Luther came to challenge its authority. They were unable to stop the separation of the English Catholic Church, and the conversion of many Catholics to Protestantism.

In 1532 the Médici family acquired the hereditary title of grand duke of **Tuscany**; for the first time in their long history, they became the rulers of Florence in name as well as fact. The family line of Cosimo became extinct in 1537; the title passed to Cosimo I (1519–1574) who was descended from Giovanni di Bicci's other son, Lorenzo (1395–1440). Thus, the "younger" family branch came to power.

The Médicis also provided a queen of France. **Catherine de Médici** (1519–1589) married the Duke of Orléans who later became King Henry II. Her three sons all served as kings; her vigilant leadership preserved the French monarchy during the turmoil of the religious wars of the 16th century.

Lorenzo the Magnificent

For nearly a thousand years, the emperor of Japan was strictly a figurehead and a shogun held the ruling power. That period came to an end with the reign of Mutsuhito, whose throne name was Meiji Tenno.

In 1867 a group of radical young Japanese leaders overthrew the shogunate and placed 15-year-old Emperor **Mutsuhito** (1852–1912) on the throne. To symbolize the start of a new era, Emperor Mutsuhito moved the imperial capital from Kyoto to the modern city of Tokyo.

Strong and forceful in personality, the new emperor led the modernization of Japan. During his reign (1867–1912), Mutsuhito declared a new constitution, imported European advisers, changed the Japanese army from a feudal to a modern one, and created the new Japanese navy.

Mutsuhito's son, Emperor **Yoshihito** (reigned 1912–1926), brought Japan into World War I. He continued the modernization work begun by his father. He was succeeded by his son **Hirohito** (reigned 1926–1989), who had traveled in Europe when he was the crown prince. Retiring and scholarly in nature, he was an expert in marine biology, which remained his true passion throughout his life. Historians are not certain whether Emperor Hirohito was active in the Japanese planning that led to

Emperor Hirohito

the war with China in 1937, or Japan's entry into **World War II** in 1941. He may have been a puppet emperor at that point, or he may have promoted the desires of the militaristic party headed by General **Hideki Tojo**.

After the United States dropped two atomic bombs on Japan, Hirohito made a radio broadcast to his people on August 15, 1945. He declared that he and Japan had made a great mistake in entering the war and that he would seek peace immediately. This was the first time that most Japanese had ever heard their emperor's voice—the traditional belief that the emperor was a god soon came to an end.

The Japanese clearly wanted the emperor to remain on the throne; that was the only concession they managed to obtain from the Allies before they surrendered. However, the new Japanese constitution of 1947 gave the country a constitutional government and made the emperor's role largely ceremonial.

Hirohito remained emperor until his death. His son **Akihito** (b. 1933) took the throne in 1989. In 1959, he became the first Japanese emperor to marry a commoner, when he wed Shoda Michiko.

After the conquests of Genghis Khan and Kublai Khan, China was ruled by the foreign Yuan dynasty. These Mongol rulers were overthrown and replaced by a peasant family, the Mings, that reasserted the right of the Chinese to be governed by their own people.

The first Ming ruler, **Chu Yuan-chang** (1328–1398), was born to an impoverished peasant family in Anhwei. Orphaned at 16, he entered a monastery, and then wandered the countryside as a beggar for several years. He sensed that his people were weary of Mongol rule and wanted a change in government. In 1352 he joined a rebel force, and by 1355 he had become leader of an entire rebel army.

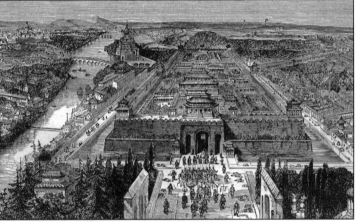

View of Peking

Chu Yuan-chang led his forces in the capture of the city of **Nanking** in 1356. Although this was a great victory, it took another long 12 years before he could capture Peking and expel the Mongol lords. In 1368 he made Nanking the capital and placed himself on the throne with the name Ming T'ai Tsu.

Ming T'ai Tsu was an able ruler. He unified China by reconquering the province of Yunnan. He restored the ancient system of examinations—based on Confucian principles—for entrance to the imperial bureaucracy. This re-created a class of scholar-officials who became the backbone of the **Ming** dynasty. On the negative side, he abolished the post of prime minister and ruled with great severity.

Ming T'ai Tsu was succeeded by his nephew in 1398, but he was soon ousted from the throne by **Yung Lo** ("Perpetual Happiness") who reigned from 1402 to 1424. Yung Lo led five massive military expeditions deep into central Asia and reduced the last threat of Mongol invasions. By this time, the Chinese armies were organized enough to withstand any future attacks. He also sent maritime expeditions as far as the Persian Gulf and east Africa. This has led scholars to ponder whether China might have eventually "discovered" Europe and the Americas before it was itself "discovered" by people from the West. These expeditions ceased after the reign of Yung Lo.

Peking (present-day Beijing) became the primary capital of the Ming rulers in 1421. After the death of Yung Lo, a gradual decline set in. The Ming emperors came increasingly to rely on the advice of eunuchs who fought bitterly with the scholar-officials over policy.

China's agriculture flourished during the Ming period. Peanuts, maize, and sweet potatoes first appeared in China during this time, and the Chinese population soared from around 65 million at the start of the Ming period to nearly 150 million by its close.

Mogul Dynasty
Indian rulers

The fabulously wealthy and successful Mogul (Mughal) family ruled much of India for more than a century.

Of noble Turkish and Asian blood, the founder of the dynasty, **Babur** (1483–1530), left central Asia and invaded India in 1526; by 1529 he had overwhelmed the forces of the Delhi sultanate, and created his own kingdom in north and central India.

Babur

His son **Humayun** (1508–1556) succeeded him. Fascinated by astrology and perhaps addicted to opium, Humayun was forced off the throne by Sher Khan, an Afghan chief who had previously served Babur. Humayan fled to Persia; on the way, his wife gave birth to their son Akbar (1542–1605), the leader who would later recover the family fortunes.

Humayun regained his throne in 1555, but he died the following year, leaving the leadership to **Akbar**. The young monarch decided to work within, rather than against, India's racially and religiously diverse society. Though his family was Moslem, Akbar abolished the burdensome taxes on India's Hindu citizens. He divided his kingdom into 12 provinces and governed them with justice and reason. Akbar also sponsored Indian art and architecture that combined Persian and Islamic influences.

The revolt of one of his sons darkened Akbar's later years. He was succeeded by **Jahangir** (1569–1627), who took the name of Nur Jahan ("Light of the World"). Jahangir and his son Khurram (1592–1666), who renamed himself Shah Jahan ("Emperor of the World"), were also great patrons of art and architecture. When his beloved wife Mumatz Mahal (who had given birth to 14 children) died, Shah Jahan set thousands of workers to the task of building a tomb in her honor. The structure would become the **Taj Mahal**, one of the great architectural wonders of the world.

Shah Jahan's son Aurangzeb (1658–1707) renamed himself **Almagir** ("World Conqueror"). A stern and very pious man, he undid much of Akbar's work creating a climate of religious tolerance. Almagir imposed special taxes on Hindu citizens, and equality between Moslems and Hindus ended. Seeking to fulfill the name he had given himself, Almagir attempted to conquer central and southern **India**. He won many victories, but the cost to his people was horrendous. The expense of moving his capital (500,000 people, 50,000 camels, and 30,000 elephants) during military campaigns exhausted the state resources.

Following Almagir, the Mogul state fell into confusion and disarray. Although a Mogul state existed until 1858, when the British dissolved it, the cohesive leadership that the rulers of one remarkable family provided was never repeated.

For more than 125 years, the Aztecs ruled Mexico through a succession of leaders, the most famous of whom surrendered power only because he mistook a Spanish conqueror for a legendary God.

According to their own legends, the Aztecs migrated to the Valley of Mexico and, in around 1325 , a war God they called Huitzilopochtli told them to build a city on an island in Lake Texcoco. They named this city **Tenochtitlan**. As the Aztecs gained wealth and power, Tenochtitlan became one of the most magnificent cities in the world.

Acamapichtli was the first Aztec leader. He died in 1396 and was followed by three successors who ruled for relatively brief periods.

Itzcoatl (reigned 1428–1440)—the fifth Aztec speaker—was a formidable ruler. During his reign, the Aztecs truly became an imperial people. He gathered other small city-states into an alliance and overthrew the rule of the neighboring city of Azcapotzalco. Instead of leaving the small city-states to live in peace, Itzcoatl and his remarkable foreign minister—his nephew Tlacelel—sought expansion at any cost. At the height of its empire, the Aztecs had as many as 11 million Indian subjects under their rule.

When Itzcoatl died, the new leader was Motecuhzoma Ilhuicamina (reigned 1440–1468), known as **Montezuma I**.

During the early 1450s, the Aztecs suffered a series of natural disasters that ruined their crops. They turned to human sacrifice to appease the gods, especially the war god. When this method appeared to be successful, they began systematic conquests of neighboring Indian tribes; their chief objective was the taking of live captives to use for sacrifices. Thousands of foreigners were sacrificed in the Aztec temples beginning in 1450.

In 1502, Motecuhzoma Xocoyotzin—known as Emperor **Montezuma II**—came to power. In 1519 an army of 600 Spaniards arrived in Tenochtitlan, led by **Hernàn Cortés.** The Aztecs were amazed at the Spaniards, who had arrived in "white-winged ships," and came equipped with horses, steel swords and armor, and light artillery. Montezuma believed that Cortés might be Quetzacoatl, an Aztec god who had once ruled their lands, vanished mysteriously, and had promised to return from the east. Montezuma feared Cortés and allowed him and his men to enter the city. The Spaniards abducted and later killed him.

Montezuma's nephew **Cuauhtemoc** (reigned 1520–1521), carried on the fight. He rallied the people of Tenochtitlan and fought valiantly against the Spaniards and their Indian allies, and drove them away. However, a year later Cortés returned with a huge army, and captured and destroyed Tenochtitlan, and executed Cuauhtemoc.

Montezuma II

One of the few royal families of Europe to still hold its crown is the House of Orange-Nassau in the **Netherlands**. The devotion and attachment of the Dutch people to their monarchy can be traced through the history of two families.

William of Nassau

During the 12th century, the counts of Orange were *vassals* (feudal tenants) of the Holy Roman Emperor. Their lands were on the banks of the Rhone River, very close to Avignon in southern France. By the 13th century, they acquired the title of "princes" of **Orange**. Then in 1530, Prince René of Orange added the principality of Orange to his father's family holdings in Germany (including Nassau) and joined the two families of Nassau and Orange.

William (1533–84), count of Orange and Nassau, was born in Germany, but he made the Netherlands his home. He and his ancestors became leaders of *stadholders* (hereditary magistrates). Because Spain possessed the Netherlands at the time, William led an independence movement against the **Hapsburg** monarchy of Spain. His political skills earned him the nickname of "William the Silent." Determined to crush the revolt, King Philip II of Spain put a large price on William's head. In 1584, an assassin succeeded in killing William at his home.

The Dutch independence movement gained strength, with William as a martyr to the cause. His son, Maurice of Nassau (reigned 1584-1625), was a skillful military leader who fought the Spanish off and on during the **Eighty Years' War** between the two countries. Maurice's brother, Frederick Henry (reigned 1625-1647) succeeded him.

Leadership of the House of Orange-Nassau passed to Frederick Henry's 23 year-old son, **William II** (reigned 1647–50); his early death created a period of instability, and Dutch wars with England and France later followed. Finally, in 1672, William III (reigned 1672–1702), the son of William II, assumed control.

William III crossed the English Channel to conquer England during the Glorious Revolution of 1688. His victory over his father-in-law King James II at the Battle of the Boyne in Ireland in 1690 gave his family name to the "Orangemen" of Northern Ireland today. William had the unique distinction of being the only person ever to rule both England and the Netherlands. After his death, the House of Orange-Nassau returned to the Netherlands permanently.

William I (reigned 1813–1840)—a distant relative of William III—became the first king of the Netherlands in 1814. By the late 19th century, the throne had passed to his great granddaughter , Queen **Wilhelmina** (reigned 1890–1948). She kept up the hopes of her countryman and maintained the family monarchy during World Wars I and II by sending regular radio broadcasts from England. She returned home in 1945, but abdicated the throne in 1948 in favor of her daughter Juliana (b. 1909). A very popular queen, Juliana herself chose to abdicate the throne to her daughter Beatrix Wilhelmina Armgard (b. 1938), who continued to rule throughout the rest of the century.

The family that dominated 20th-century Argentine politics began humbly. **Juan Domingo Perón** (1895–1974) was born out of wedlock to a Native American girl and a white father who managed a sheep ranch. Perón attended military school and was commissioned a lieutenant in 1915.

Perón was sent as military attaché to Italy in 1938; there he experienced and approved of the fascist governments of both Mussolini and Hitler. In June 1943, Perón masterminded a successful military coup in **Argentina** and became the power behind the dictator, rising to vice president in 1944.

Perón was deposed and briefly jailed by another military coup in October, 1945, but his supporters won his release. In doing so, they heeded the call of Maria Eva Duarte, Perón's mistress. She had mobilized the Descamisados ("shirtless ones") of the Argentine labor unions and was a powerful political ally to Perón. Upon winning his freedom, he married Maria, who soon became known as "Evita."

Maria Eva Duarte de Perón (1919–52) was the fifth illegitimate child of a landowner. She went to Buenos Aires at the age of 15 and enjoyed modest success as a soap-opera radio actress. She met Colonel Perón in 1944.

Juan Perón became president of Argentina in 1946 and appointed his wife minister of labor. As the "eyes and ears" of her husband, she completely purged the unions of all leaders who were hostile to him. Evita toured Spain, France, and Italy and became an important political figure in her own right. Soon after her death from cancer, a legend developed that she was in some ways an Argentine "Joan of Arc" who had sacrificed her life for her country.

Juan Perón was forced to resign the presidency by another military coup in 1955. He went into exile in other South American nations before he settled in Spain in 1960. There he married **Maria Estela Martinez** (b. 1931), who became known as "Isabel" Perón. The couple made a sensational return to Argentina in 1973. Juan and Isabel ran for president and vice president; they won the election with 62% of the vote.

The Peróns wrestled with, but could not tame, the demon of runaway inflation in Argentina during the 1970s. By the time of his death from heart disease in 1974, Juan Perón was under increasing pressure to solve the country's problems. When he died, Isabel replaced him as president and governed until a military coup deposed her in 1976. She was kept under house arrest until 1981, when she was allowed to return to Spain. The Argentine government pardoned her in 1983.

Eva Duarte de Perón

Using considerable political skill and influence, the Pitt family brought Great Britain to the peak of world greatness and power.

Thomas "Diamond" Pitt (1653–1726) was a British merchant who became interested in India during the time of the Mogul dynasty. Pitt broke Britain's trading rules with India by doing business outside the control of the British East India Company. He was arrested and fined, but by 1694 the company found it was simpler to employ him than to compete against him.

In 1709, Thomas Pitt returned to England a very wealthy man, and he became a member of **Parliament,** representing the manor of Old Sarum. At home, Pitt was a tyrant. The only family member he favored was his grandson William, whose father Robert Pitt had also served in the House of Commons.

William Pitt (1708–1778) attended, but did not graduate from, Eton College. Pitt became famous for his oratorical skills after he entered Parliament in 1735. In 1754 he married Lady Hester Grenville, and they were a devoted and happy couple throughout their marriage.

For a number of years, Pitt remained outside the cabinet decision-making process because King **George II** disliked him intensely. However, Great Britain suffered several defeats at the beginning of the Seven Years' War (1756-1763) that created a leadership

William Pitt

crisis, and Pitt's political influence began to rise. Finally, in December, 1757, King George relented, and Pitt became minister of foreign affairs.

Pitt directed a stunning turnaround in the war. He sent money to Prussia, enabling it to tie up French military strength in Europe. Then he sent large British fleets and armies overseas to attack French colonial possessions. The Pitt strategy yielded tremendous gains. The year 1759 became known as the Year of Victories. Britain's victory over France was accomplished through the victories of military leaders that Pitt promoted and nurtured.

Pitt was removed from office in 1761. He made a political comeback and served again as prime minister from 1766–1768, but the days of his real power were gone. After his death, parliamentary leadership passed to his son, **William Pitt** "the Younger" (1759–1806). He became chancellor of the exchequer in 1782 and served twice as prime minister (1783–1801 and 1804–6).

The younger William faced a more formidable situation than his father had. The military strength of Napoleonic France severely tested his leadership and all the resources of the **British Empire**. Still, Britain's survival during the early Napoleonic years owed much to the diplomacy and strategy of William Pitt the Younger. His death ended the Pitt political dynasty.

Plantagenet
English monarchs

Richard 1

One of the most influential English ruling families, the House of Plantagenet controlled England's destiny for nearly 250 years.

Henry II (reigned 1154–1189) was the first of the Plantagenet family to rule England and its possessions in France and Ireland. He came to the throne as a compromise candidate, to appease the two factions that had fought each other for a generation.

Henry married **Eleanor of Acquitaine**, a great leader in her own right; the two were alternately loving and quarrelsome. Henry greatly expanded the size of the Plantagenet domain; he invaded Ireland and gained new family holdings in France. His desire to control Acquitaine was one of the disagreements between him and his wife.

Beginning in 1173, Henry fell victim to the plots and intrigues of his numerous sons—who were supported by their mother, Eleanor. When he died in 1189, Henry was struggling to hold onto the large Plantagenet empire he had created.

Henry's successor, his son, **Richard I** (reigned 1189–1199), known as "the Lion-Hearted," was a skillful and daring warrior, but no administrator. He spent nearly all of his 10-year reign on the European continent as leader of the Third Crusade against the Moslems. Richard died while fighting in France.

John (reigned 1199–1216) succeeded his older, more popular brother. There was little of the soldier in him, but he was a capable administrator. Drawn into conflicts with both the pope and King Philip Augustus of France, John stumbled badly. He lost Normandy, Anjou, and Acquitaine to France.

Infuriated by these humiliations, a number of English barons brought John to a meadow at Runnymede, outside of London, and forced him to sign the *Magna Carta* (Great Charter). Although it has been called a democratic document, the charter actually sought to reconfirm the ancient feudal rights of the barons.

John's son, **Henry III** (reigned 1216-1272) succeeded him. His rule was marked by the strong influence of the pope, and the outbreak of civil war that briefly toppled him from power.

Henry's son, Edward I (reigned 1272–1307), claimed the principality of Wales, and fought both Scotland and France. Edward II (reigned 1307–1327) lacked his father's ruthlessness and skill. His son, Edward III (reigned 1327–1377), pressed his family's right to rule France. He won major battles at the start of the **Hundred Years' War**, but was unable to capture Paris.

Richard II (reigned 1377–1400) was the last Plantagenet king. He resigned his crown in 1400 and died in captivity, a prisoner of King Henry IV, the first ruler from the new House of Lancaster (see no. 59).

The ancient Roman family of Pliny gathered the teachings of past civilizations for the benefit of scholars and scientists of future generations.

Gaius Plinius Secundus (c. A.D. 23–79) came from a prosperous family in northern Italy. He went to Rome as a young man and served in the Roman army and then as prefect (magistrate) of the cavalry in Germany.

Pliny went into semi-retirement in A.D. 65. He held the important post of procurator of Spain (A.D. 65–70), but spent most of his energy on the collection and analysis of old Greek texts.

Roman Emperor Trajan

Like the rest of the **Roman** aristocracy, Pliny admired the learning of the ancient Greeks. He decided to preserve all the knowledge he had collected from Greek texts in Latin. He produced *Bella Germanica*, a 20-volume work that described the wars between the Germans and Romans. His three-volume *Studiosus* described the proper training of an orator, an important job for any Roman who aspired to leadership. He also wrote a a 31-volume history of the Roman world.

Pliny's greatest work was his 37-volume *Historia naturalis* (Natural History). Citing his sources carefully, he covered the physical universe, geology, ethnology, anthropology, zoology, botany, pharmacology, and mineralogy and metallurgy.

Pliny became prefect of the Roman fleet in Naples; on August 24, A.D. 79, he went ashore to investigate an unusual cloud formation that was frightening the local inhabitants. Pliny died of asphyxiation caused by these poisonous fumes—they had come from the volcano erupting above **Pompeii**.

Pliny's nephew and adopted son, Gaius Plinius Caecilius Secundus (c. A.D. 61–114) became known as **Pliny the Younger**. He studied and practiced law in Rome, and rose through merit to the honored rank of consul in A.D. 100. In A.D. 112, he was appointed governor of Bithynia and Pontus (in present-day Turkey). He died two years later, while serving on this assignment.

Pliny the Younger left behind his major work, the *Epistulae,* which consisted of letters to and from friends, and his official correspondence with Emperor Trajan. Pliny showed great literary style, although he did not possess his uncle's sophistication.

The works of Pliny the Elder and Younger were preserved in the Roman archives for centuries. During the **Middle Ages**, when Greek learning was largely lost, scholars turned to the works of Pliny the Elder for answers in science and mathematics. Not until about 1500, when a number of Greek texts were recovered, was Pliny replaced as the key source for scholarship.

By bringing the riches of far-off Asia to Europe, the Polo family of Venice helped pave the way for the cultural expansions of the Renaissance.

During the mid-13th century, Niccolò and Maffeo Polo were prosperous long-distance traders from **Venice** who traveled to Constantinople and then Mongol Russia to develop new trade networks. War prevented the Polos from returning directly home, so they traveled eastward until they could circle around Asia Minor (present-day Turkey). In fact, the intrepid brothers went all the way to China, which they called Cathay.

At that time, the Mongol **Kublai Khan** (see no. 38) sat on throne of China. He received the brothers with courtesy and was curious to learn about the Christian West. When he finally allowed them to leave, he asked them to return and to bring 100 Christian priests and some of the sacred oil from Jerusalem.

The Polo brothers returned to Venice in 1269. Niccolò's son **Marco Polo** (1254–1324) pleaded with his father and uncle to take him on their return trip to China and they relented. The three Polos left Venice in 1271.

They journeyed for three and a half years before they finally reached Kublai Khan's summer capital of Shangtu, later called "Xanadu." There, the Polos became honored members of the Khan's enormous court. Kublai Khan took a particular liking to Marco, who became one of his trusted advisers.

Many years passed. The Polos became anxious to return to their homeland, but the Khan would not allow them to leave. He was fond of all three of them, but had especially come to rely on Marco. In 1292, the Khan finally gave the Polos permission to depart. They traveled by water across the Indian Ocean, landed in the **Persian Gulf**, and jour-

Marco Polo

neyed the rest of the way on foot.

The Polos arrived in Venice in 1295. After an absence of 24 years, no one recognized them; so the Polos hosted a huge party. At a critical moment in the entertainment, the Polos cut the seams of their garments; gold and jewels spilled onto the floor, indicating that wherever they had been, they had found great wealth.

Marco Polo was captured in a sea battle against Genoese ships a few years later. While in captivity, he dictated the story of his journeys to a man named **Rustichello**, who wrote *Description of the World* based on what Marco had told him. The book contained many exaggerations, but there seems little doubt, that the Polos had indeed reached China and returned—a feat accomplished by no other European of their time.

79. Ptolemy
Egyptian rulers

Octavian and Cleopatra

Egypt has had more political dynasties than any other country. While the pharaohs who built the pyramids had a great impact on Egyptian history, perhaps the most famous Egyptian leader, Cleopatra, belonged to what was actually a foreign dynasty—the Ptolemys.

On his deathbed, **Alexander the Great** was asked who should inherit his vast empire. Supposedly he answered, "To the strongest!" No one king or emperor emerged as ruler after his death; instead, his best generals divided up his conquests among themselves. One of those generals was Soter (c. 367–c. 282 B.C.), who became the satrap, or military ruler, of Egypt.

Once he was familiar with Egypt's history and culture, Soter became bold enough to declare himself King **Ptolemy I** in 305 B.C. He thereby started the 33rd dynasty of pharaohs. It was during the reign of his grandson, Ptolemy III (246–221 B.C.), that

the kingdom reached its apex. Ptolemy III conquered the kingdom in Syria, and Egypt swelled to the point where it was once again nearly an empire. It capital, Alexandria, became the center for learning in the Mediterranean world, replacing even Athens.

A long decline began during the reign of **Ptolemy IV** (222–204 B.C.). Corruption within the kingdom and a new array of foreign enemies threatened what was the most successful remnant from the empire of Alexander the Great. The Ptolemies had to fight hard to keep Phoenicia and Palestine; they were in fact conquered by King Antiochus, but pressure from a new great power—that of Rome—forced Antiochus away from Egypt.

The Ptolemies continued to decline and their kingdom became something of a client kingdom of Rome. During the time of Julius Caesar (100–44 B.C.), Roman troops first arrived in Egypt in pursuit of Caesar's rival Pompey, whom they captured and beheaded. Caesar could easily have annexed Egypt, but his attraction to **Cleopatra VII** (69–30 B.C.) prevented him. She persuaded Caesar to defeat her rival for the throne, her brother, Ptolemy XIII (63–47 B.C.). After his death, she became queen of Egypt (reigned 47-30 B.C.).

Caesar returned to Rome and was assassinated in 44 B.C. Cleopatra then managed to seduce and control **Mark Antony**, one of Caesar's lieutenants. The couple formed a power base in the eastern Mediterranean. However, **Octavian** (later known as Caesar Augustus) defeated Antony and Cleopatra at the Battle of Actium in 31 B.C. to command complete control of the Egyptian kingdom. Rather than surrender to what she knew would be a humiliating spectacle as a prisoner in Rome, Cleopatra chose to poison herself by the bite of a snake. Octavian annexed Egypt after her death.

A young man from a family of farmers became one of the wealthiest men of the 20th century—and left a family legacy of philanthropy and political activism.

John Davison Rockefeller was born on a farm in Richford, New York, in 1839. In 1862 he and a partner invested $4,000 in a company that devised a method for cleaning crude oil. By 1867, he was the major owner of the firm—called Rockefeller, Andrews and Flagler.

Rockefeller worked tirelessly to centralize the oil business. He wanted to bring all methods of production and transportation under one business umbrella—his own. He incorporated **Standard Oil Company** in 1870, which became Standard Oil Company of New Jersey in 1899. With his success came criticism; he was condemned by many for squelching all competition and gaining a virtual lock on the entire American oil industry. The federal government successfully sued the company in 1911 for violation of the anti-trust laws; the U.S. Supreme Court ruled Standard Oil was a monopoly and had to be dissolved.

This legal setback did not impede Rockefeller's enormous success. He made hundreds of millions of dollars by the time World War I began; in his later years, he turned to philanthropy, giving millions away to charitable and educational enterprises. He died in 1937.

His only son, **John D. Rockefeller, Jr.** (1874–1960), worked in his father's business, and like his father, turned to philanthropy after World War I. He started the fund to restore Colonial Williamsburg in Virginia and donated a $9 million plot of land for the building of the **United Nations** in New York City. Through his marriage to Abby Aldrich, he had one daughter and five sons.

John D. Rockefeller III (1906–78) served as chairman of the board of the Rockefeller Foundation. His brother **Nelson Aldrich Rockefeller** (1908–79) entered politics during the 1950s. He served as governor of New York for four terms (1959–73). He also made three failed attempts to win the Republican presidential nomination, in 1960, 1964, and 1968. He finally won the consolation prize; President Gerald R. Ford named him vice-president in 1974.

Winthrop Rockefeller (1912–73) was governor of Arkansas between 1967 and 1971. His son, Winthrop P. Rockefeller, became lieutenant governor of the same state in 1996. John D. III's son, **John Davison Rockefeller IV** (b.1937), better known as "Jay," served in the U.S. State Department. Then he became governor of West Virginia (1976–84). He won election to the U.S. Senate in 1984 where he stood out as a vigorous advocate of working-class Americans.

Nelson Rockefeller

Best known for their dramatic fall from power during the Russian Revolution, the Romanov family ruled Czarist Russia for 300 years.

The family came to the throne after a 20-year period that the Russians called the "Time of Troubles." In 1613 an Assembly of the Land, composed of 500 delegates, voted **Mikhail Feodorovich Romanov** (1596–1645) to be the "Czar and Autocrat of All the Russias."

Mikhail was succeeded by his son, but it was his grandson, Czar **Peter the Great** (reigned 1682–1725) who set Russia on a new course. Peter built the first Russian navy and contested ownership of the Baltic and Black seas with Sweden and Turkey. He built a new capital—strongly influenced by the great capitals of Western Europe—along the Baltic Sea and called it St. Petersburg. Peter also did much to encourage trade, industry, and education.

From the time of Peter's death until the 1760s, various Romanovs held the throne for brief periods. Then in 1762, the widow of Peter's grandson, Peter III, succeeded to the throne. Of German ancestry, Czarina **Catherine the Great**, (reigned 1762–1796) was as ambitious as Peter the Great had been. She brought the European Enlightenment to Russia, and greatly expanded Russia's territory by annexing Poland and the Crimea.

Catherine's son, Paul (reigned 1796-1801) was mentally unbalanced, and was assassinated in a palace revolt. He was succeeded by his son, **Alexander I** (reigned 1801–1825), who was best known for resisting the Napoleonic invasion of 1812.

Alexander's brother, Czar **Nicholas I** (reigned 1825–1855), became known as "the Policeman of Europe," because he often dispatched Russian troops to put down popular revolts in other nations. His son, Alexander II (reigned 1855–1881) officially freed the Russian serfs in

1861. Ironically, his liberalization was halted when he was assassinated by a bomb.

Alexander's son, Czar Alexander III (reigned 1881–1894) was both repressive and unimaginative. His son, Czar **Nicholas II** (reigned 1894–1917) was a reluctant czar. Devoted to his wife, his family, and especially his hemophiliac son, he allowed himself to be influenced by the intrigues of **Rasputin**, a self-proclaimed "holy man" who reportedly could control the bleeding of the young

Nicholas II and family

Czarevich. However, what proved to be Nicholas's undoing, was his decision to enter World War I.

The war was a calamity for Russia. Several million Russians were killed or wounded; soldiers fought without proper equipment or even shoes. In 1917 a revolt in St. Petersburg quickly spread to Moscow and other cities. Nicholas abdicated the throne, but it was too late. Later that year, the communists—led by Vladimir Lenin—seized power. In 1918, they killed Nicholas and his entire family, bringing a violent end to the Romanov dynasty.

82. Roosevelt
American politicians

The family that produced two of the greatest American presidents was originally Dutch. The Roosevelts migrated to New Netherland, which became New York in 1664, and thrived as farmers on the fertile fields along the Hudson River.

By the time **Theodore Roosevelt** (1858-1919) was born, the family was wealthy and living in New York City. Theodore was educated at Harvard University and Columbia Law School. He married in 1880, but his wife died in 1884; he then went west to work on a cattle ranch in the Dakota Territory. Roosevelt returned east and entered politics as a reform-minded Republican. He married again, to Edith Carow, and the couple had six children.

President McKinley appointed Roosevelt assistant secretary of the navy in 1897; he resigned his post the next year to fight in the **Spanish-American War**. He won fame through his leadership of the "Rough Riders" cavalry unit. Popular appeal catapulted him to the vice-presidency in 1901, and succeeded to the presidency when President McKinley was assassinated that year.

As president, Roosevelt broke up corporate monopolies, and advocated strong conservationism of natural resources. He served two terms (1901–9) and ran for a third in 1912 at the head of the Bull Moose Party, but was defeated.

While he was president, Theodore gave away his niece Eleanor Roosevelt (1884–1962) in marriage to her fifth cousin, **Franklin Delano Roosevelt** (1882–1945). Franklin entered politics as a New York state senator in 1910, and later served as assistant secretary of the navy. Stricken with polio in 1921, he overcame his illness to become New York's governor in 1928. In 1932, he won the presidency, as the nation was in the worst throes of the Great Depression.

The second Roosevelt president—known to

FDR and family

the nation as FDR—was a Democrat. He worked with great energy to combat the misery of the **Depression**, creating government agencies to put people to work. Loved by millions of Americans and reviled by more than a few, Roosevelt won election an unprecedented four times—1932, 1936, 1940, and 1944. During his third and fourth terms, he steered America through the difficult days of **World War II**. Roosevelt delegated authority superbly; he surrounded himself with remarkable men who carried out his policies, but who always remembered that F.D.R. was the boss.

Even so, Roosevelt's impact would have been less without the backing of his remarkable wife, Eleanor. She traveled widely, gathered information first-hand, and became the spokesperson for the poor and disadvantaged in American society. She was far ahead of her time in her work for civil rights for all Americans.

Two of Franklin and Eleanor's sons—James Roosevelt and Franklin Roosevelt Jr. served in the U.S. House of Representatives.

From the Jewish ghetto of Frankfurt, Germany, one banking family rose to wealth and power—the Rothschilds.

Mayer Amschel Rothschild (1744–1812) grew up on "Jew Street" in Frankfurt, which was then part of the Holy Roman Empire. He first studied to become a rabbi, but switched to an apprenticeship in banking. He began his career modestly, selling coins and heirlooms to wealthy nobles of the principality of Hesse-Cassel.

Mayer married Gutele Schnapper in 1769. The couple had five sons: Amschel Mayer (1773–1855), Salomon (1774–1855), Nathan (1777–1836), Karl (1788–1855), and Jakob (1792–1868) who was called James. Using his large family as messengers and salesmen, Mayer Amschel became a court factor (exchanger of money) for Prince William of Hanau. When Prince William became the landgrave (ruler) of **Hesse-Cassel** in 1785, the Rothschilds became his principal source of credit.

In 1804, the Rothschilds made their first major loan to a foreign government— Denmark. The family appeared to suffer a major setback when Napoleon conquered Hesse-Cassel in 1806. Actually, the Rothschilds took advantage of the Napoleonic wars. Nathan went to London, Salomon founded the family branch in **Vienna**, James went to Paris, and Karl became the foremost banker in Naples.

Although all of the brothers were successful in business, Nathan made the largest financial gain. Learning that **Napoleon** had been defeated at the Battle of Waterloo (1815), Nathan conspicuously dumped all his shares in British government stocks on the London stock exchange. Believing that Nathan knew that Napoleon had won, eager investors sold their shares in the stocks as well. At the last possible moment, Nathan repurchased the stocks at a fraction of the price. In one day, he had assured the family's fortune.

Baron Lionel de Rothschild

After the Napoleonic wars, the brothers found greater financial success. They followed two basic family rules: Always keep the business within the family, and never seek exorbitant profits. These principles enabled the brothers to weather and even profit from the instability caused by the revolutions of 1830 and 1848.

Mayer's grandsons continued the family tradition. Nathan's son, Lionel not only succeeded his father as manager of the family's London branch; he entered politics as well. He became the first Jewish Member of **Parliament** in 1852, and served there until 1874. Two other grandsons—Alfonse and Amschel—managed family branches in Paris and Vienna.

During the 20th century, Baron Guy de Rothschild ran the Paris branch, and Nathaniel Mayer, the third British baron of Rothschild, ran the **London** office. Although the family suffered greatly from the anti-Semitism of World War II, the Rothschilds continued to play an important role in European finances.

84. Sa'ud
Saudi Arabian rulers

Since the early 18th century, the House of Sa'ud has provided 13 ruling princes (*emirs*) in regions of the Arabian peninsula, and 5 absolute monarchs of the kingdom of **Saudi Arabia.**

The Arabian Desert was a no-man's-land in the 18th century; the Ottoman Empire and the Wahhabi religious movement—which sought to bring purity back to Islam—fought over the area. Out of this strife and confusion, **Sa'ud I** (reigned c. 1720–1726) became the first known family leader in Arabia and the emir of Nejd. Four family members succeeded him until Egypt briefly took over the realm (1818–23).

Turki (reigned 1823–1834), son of the last Sa'ud emir before Egyptian rule, started a second Sa'ud dynasty. By 1865 the family controlled most of noncoastal Arabia. Internal dissension, however, weakened the family and in 1891, the Sa'ud capital, Riyadh, fell to the rival house of Rashid, which was based in the northern city of Hail. The Saud family took refuge in British-protected Kuwait.

Abd al-Aziz (c. 1880–1953) was 14 when he went into exile. In 1902 he led a small band of followers to recapture Riyadh. His rival, Abd al-Aziz ibn Rashid, asked for and received help from Constantinople—eight Turkish battalions came to his support. In 1905, Abd al-Aziz defeated his joint foes at the Battle of Bukaiyra and the Turks withdrew.

Abd al-Aziz soon confronted another foe: Hussain ibn Ali al-Hashem, the ruler of **Mecca**. Abd al-Aziz sponsored a second Wahhabi movement against Hussain. He also won official recognition of his rule by the British government.

During World War I, Hussain declared himself "King of All Arabs" and fought with the British in their drive against the Ottoman Turks. Abd al-Aziz sat on the sidelines during the war, but then came forward against Hussain. First Mecca and then Medina surrendered to Abd al-Aziz and Hussain fled to Cyprus. By 1925 Abd al-Aziz was the master of the Arabian peninsula, with the title of emir of Nejd. In 1932 he elevated himself to king and changed the name of his country to Saudi Arabia. Three years later, geologists discovered vast oil fields beneath the desert; suddenly Saudi Arabia became very important in international politics.

After Abd al-Aziz's death, his younger brother took the throne as King **Saud IV** (reigned 1953–1964). His family deposed him in 1964 and replaced him with another younger brother, King Faisal II (reigned 1964-1975). After his death, he was followed by King Khalid II (reigned 1975–82) and King **Fahd ibn Abd al-Aziz** (reigned 1982-present).

During the 40 years that followed the death of Abd al-Aziz, Saudi Arabia became a clearly recognized power in the Middle East.

Abd al-Aziz ibn Saud

Scipio and Hannibal at Zama

The Scipios were already a noble Roman family with an illustrious history when the Second Punic War began in 219 B.C.

Publius Cornelius Scipio (c. 265–211 B.C.) was one of the two Romans appointed *consul* (ruling magistrate) that year. He marched his army to northern Italy and confronted the army of Carthaginians and Gauls led by **Hannibal Barca** (see no. 6). To the surprise of most Romans, Scipio was defeated at the Battle of Ticinius River, although his son saved his life.

Publius Cornelius Scipio II (c. 233–c. 183 B.C.) became a prominent military leader at a young age. He rallied the shattered remnants of the Roman armies after the crushing defeat at the Battle of Cannae in 216 B.C. He went to Carthaginian Spain in 210 B.C. and won control of the peninsula through a series of daring maneuvers and battles. He won Spanish tribes to his side and conquered Spain by 206 B.C. When he returned to Rome, he was named consul in 205 B.C. The next year, he led a Roman army to North Africa. He defeated the Carthaginians and their Numidian allies, and forced the Carthaginians to recall Hannibal from Italy.

Scipio II won the good will and the alliance of a Numidian prince, who supplied additional cavalry to the Roman army. In 202 B.C., Scipio used the Numidian allies and a newly reformed Roman legion to defeat Hannibal at the **Battle of Zama**. In Rome, he was celebrated with a full triumph and given the name "Africanus." Scipio Africanus then advised his brother Lucius in his campaign against King Antiochus III of Syria. The Romans won the war handily, but accused both Scipios of accepting bribes from the enemy. Scipio Africanus retired to his estate outside Rome and remained embittered for the rest of his life by his compatriots' ingratitude.

Publius Cornelius Aemilianus (c. 185–129 B.C.), a grandson of Scipio Africanus, fought in the Battle of Pydna in 168 B.C. and served as a military *tribune* in Spain in 151 B.C. Aemilianus was still only a junior officer when the Third (and final) Punic War began in 149 B.C. Due to his gallant leadership in early battles and his family lineage, he became commander of the Roman forces that besieged **Carthage** in 147 B.C. Scipio captured the city in 146 B.C. On his return to Rome, Scipio was celebrated with a triumph and became known as Scipio Africanus Minor ("the Younger"). A fine orator and scholar in Greek art and literature, in his later years he served as a consul in Rome.

86. Sforza
Italian military leaders

The name Sforza—meaning "the forcer," or the "strong one—was the nickname given to the leader of a band of soldiers for hire in 15th-century Italy. The name came to represent a family that accumulated much land, money, titles, and power.

Muzio Attendolo (1369–1424) was a famous *condottiere*, a leader of a band of mercenaries who roamed the countryside during the time of the Renaissance.

A man of extreme contradictions, Attendolo led his private army into many battles—and at the same time went to Mass every day. He was the most magnetic and ruthless mercenary captain of his day.

Francesco (1401–66) took his father's nickname as his own last name. Charismatic and ruthless like his father, Francesco served Duke Filipo Maria Visconti of Milan and married the duke's daughter, Bianca Maria Visconti. He conquered the March of Ancona on the Adriatic Sea in eastern Italy, and upon the death of his father-in-law, he claimed his right by marriage to become duke of **Milan**. Weary of tyrants, the Milanese people threw him out of the city and proclaimed a republic.

Sforza fought first against Venice, then persuaded the Venetians to march with him against Milan. The city surrendered to him in March 1450 after a long siege. Remarkably, he soon won the affection of his new subjects and was able to claim his title, duke of Milan.

Milan flourished during the reign of Francesco (1450–1464). He was an ardent sponsor of the arts like his friend Cosimo de Médici. Upon Francesco's death, the duchy passed to his son **Galeazzo Maria Sforza** (1444–1476), who reigned as a brutal tyrant until republican conspirators stabbed him to death.

Galeazzo's widow, Bona, ruled as regent for two years with her son Gian Galeazzo (1469–1494). Then the duchy passed to **Lodovico the Moor** (1452–1508), a younger brother of Francesco. Lodovico made himself guardian and regent of his nephew, whom he kept as a house prisoner. When Gian Galeazzo died, Lodovico became duke of Milan in his own right.

Lodovico married Beatrice d'Este in 1491. During the next six years, the couple presided over the most splendid court of the Italian Renaissance. **Leonardo da Vinci** came north and worked as the court painter and civil engineer.

It was all too good to last. The **Valois** monarchy of France invaded in 1499. Lodovico yielded the city to the French, then won it back with the help of Austrian mercenaries. He triumphed briefly, but was captured in a second invasion in 1500; Lodovico spent the last eight years of his life as a prisoner in France.

Beatrice d'Este

The area of South Africa between the Drakensburg Mountains and Indian Ocean, once called Zululand, was the home of a famous African ruler, Shaka, and his descendants.

During the early 19th century, small chiefdoms in that region began to align into different confederacies. One of the most important of these was the Mthethwa confederacy, led by the chieftain Dingiswayo. One of his top soldiers was **Shaka** (c. 1787–1828). The chieftain adopted him as a protégé, but the pupil surpassed the master. In 1816, Shaka claimed the **Zulu** chiefdom for himself.

Shaka forced young tribesmen to leave civil society and form a permanent army. He armed them with short stabbing spears and instilled in them a strict military discipline almost unknown in tribal peoples.

Having created a true army, Shaka began a series of conquests in 1818. Within a few years, he had created a single kingdom out of the tribes and confederacies between the Tugela and Pongola rivers. Shaka ruled as a despot. His word was law, and his emphasis on military matters created a nation that was maintained by use of force.

Two of Shaka's half brothers assassinated him in 1828. One brother, **Dingane** (c. 1790–1843) took over as Zulu king and tried to continue the expansion of the kingdom. British traders at Port Natal (present-day Durban, South Africa) and the appearance of Boers in his lands thwarted these efforts. The Boers—who were white settlers of Dutch descent—had marched from Capetown to create a new country.

In 1838, Dingane ceded Natal to the Boers in a treaty, but he later massacred a group of them. This action began a short war, which the Boers won in the **Battle of Blood River**. Defeated shortly afterward by his half brother Mpande, Dingane fled to Swaziland and was killed by Africans there. Mpande ruled the Zulus from 1840 until 1872.

Cetewayo (1826–1884), a grandson of Shaka, came to the Zulu throne in 1872. He tried to play off the Afrikaner Transvaal Republic against the British colony of Natal. His efforts led to a boundary dispute between the Zulus and British. A fact-finding commission reported in favor of the Zulus, whereupon the British high commissioner in Natal demanded that Cetawayo disband his army.

Cetawayo defied the British. His action led

Zulu Warriors

to the **Zulu War**. The Zulus won a great battle at Isandhlwana, before British numbers and superiority in weapons overwhelmed them. Cetawayo was captured, deposed, and exiled. The British created 13 petty states from the Zulu kingdom. Cetawayo was allowed to return to his homeland in 1883, and died the following year.

Robert L. Stevenson and family

The Stevenson family of Scotland produced several generations of engineers who built dozens of historic lighthouses—and one famous writer who created legendary tales of sea adventures.

Thomas Smith (1752-1815) became the chief engineer for the Northern (Scottish) Lighthouse Board in 1786. Working with his stepson, Robert Stevenson, Smith built 10 lighthouses in Scottish waters; some of the more colorful names were Mull of Kintyre and Little Cumbrae.

Robert Stevenson (1772-1850) succeeded his stepfather as chief engineer. He designed and built a total of 18 lighthouses, the most famous of which was Bell Rock. Located off the eastern Scottish coast, Bell Rock had claimed the hulls of perhaps thousands of ships—70 in the year 1799 alone—before Stevenson built the remarkable lighthouse on the perilous reef. It was an engineering breakthrough that made future lighthouse builders believe they could tackle almost any location.

Alan Stevenson (1807-1865) succeeded his father Robert as chief engineer in 1838. Alan designed and built the remarkable

Skerryvore Lighthouse on a reef located to miles off the west coast of Scotland, making himself as famous as his father. Alan built a total of 12 lighthouses; he also wrote a remarkable book, *Rudimentary Treatise of the History and Construction and Illumination of Lighthouses*, published in 1850.

Alan's nephew, **Robert Louis Stevenson** (1850-1894), was also the son of an engineer. However, his father wanted a career in law for his son, and Robert pursued those studies. Plagued by ill health, Robert gave up law and began to travel in search of favorable climates—and to write. After settling in California in 1880, Stevenson created such memorable tales as *Treasure Island* (1883), *Kidnapped* (1886), and *The Strange Case of Dr. Jekyll and Mr. Hyde* (1886). Stevenson continued to travel—exploring the **South Seas** before settling on the island of Samoa—and to write; many of his works reflecting his family's interest and love for the sea and those who make it their lives.

Alan's brothers, David Stevenson (1815-1886) and Thomas Stevenson (1818-1887), designed and built 29 lighthouses during their long careers. The Japanese government contracted the brothers to build a sample lighthouse and ship it across two oceans so that Japanese engineers could have a model with which to work.

Thomas Stevenson and his nephew David A. Stevenson (1854-1938) built three lighthouses together. After Thomas's death in 1887, David and Charles Stevenson (1855-1950) designed and built 25 lighthouses, the last of which was To Ness, completed in 1937. **D. Alan Stevenson** (1891-1971) combined the family traditions by writing a book on lighthouses, *The World's Lighthouses Before 1820* (1961).

Stuart
Scottish and English monarchs

The family that would produce both Scottish and English monarchs received its name from Walter Fitzalan, "the Steward" (later changed to Stewart, then Stuart) of Scotland. He married Margaret Bruce, daughter of Robert the Bruce, (Robert I, King of Scotland) in 1315 and their son became Scotland's King **Robert II** (reigned 1371–1390). Thereafter, seven kings and queens of Scotland were Stuarts; the seventh was the unfortunate Mary, Queen of Scots (1542–1587).

Mary was forced to abdicate the throne in 1567; she was then held prisoner in England. After her enemies produced evidence that proved Mary was conspiring with the pope to assassinate Queen **Elizabeth I** (her cousin), Mary was executed.

Mary's son James grew up as King James VI (reigned 1567–1625) of Scotland. When Queen Elizabeth died without an heir, James was summoned to London to become king of England as well. In 1603 he became King

Mary Stuart

James I of England.

James's reign was relatively peaceful. However, it was his son, Charles I (reigned 1625–1649), who ran into great difficulties.

Charles I attempted to rule without Parliament. Lacking funds, he was forced to summon Parliament so that the members could vote to raise money. Many arguments ensued over the way that the king was running the country, and this led to the **English Civil War** (1642–45) in which Charles and his royalist followers were defeated. Charles was arrested, tried before a Parliamentary tribunal, and executed in January, 1649. He was the first and only English king to suffer that fate.

The English people tired, however, of the Puritanical rule of Commonwealth leader **Oliver Cromwell**. In 1660, Charles II was called from exile in France to take the throne once held by his father. Charles presided over a brilliant court until 1685, but he left no direct heir to the throne. It went, therefore, to his younger brother, **James II** (reigned 1685–1688).

James tried to revive the doctrine of rule by divine right. Fearful that he might succeed, prominent English Whig leaders formed a revolt that became the Glorious Revolution of 1688. James fled to France, and took refuge at the court of King Louis XIV.

After James failed to regain his throne, his son James Edward Stuart (1688–1766), known as the "Old Pretender," tried to stir rebellion in England and Scotland; he also failed. His son, **Charles Edward Stuart** (1720–1788), the "Young Pretender," succeeded in starting a significant revolt in Scotland in 1745. However, his forces were defeated at Culloden Moor, and he escaped from Scotland and went to France. His younger brother, Henry Stuart, died in 1807, bringing the Stuart line to an end.

The Tagore family of Calcutta provided poets, writers and scholars for India during a period when the country was struggling to find its identity. Stretching from the height of the British colonial period to World War II, the Tagores became symbols of an India that yearned to be independent.

Dwarkanath Tagore was born in 1746. Known as the "Raja" prince, he acquired great wealth as a merchant. He made two trips to England and Europe and met with kings, queens, and even the pope. He had three sons: Devendranath, Girindranath, and Nagendranath.

Devendranath (1817–1905), the oldest of the brothers, married Sarada Devi; the couple had 14 children, nearly all of whom made significant contributions to Bengali and Indian culture. Devendranath excused himself from the mercantile demands that his father placed on him and became known as **Maharishi** ("Great Sage"). He translated the Rigveda and Upanishads, sacred Hindu texts, into Bengali and spent many of the last years of his life in silent meditation.

Devendranath's oldest son, Dwijendranath, became a noted writer and philosopher. His second son, Satyendranath, was a **Sanskrit** scholar; he was also the first Indian to enter the official Civil Service during the years of British rule. Jyotirindranath was a musician. Two daughters in the family were noteworthy: Saudamini was her father's beloved caretaker, and Swarnakumari Devi became the first female Bengali novelist.

Rabindranath Tagore (1861–1941), the youngest of Devendranath's children, endured an upbringing in which the household servants and his schoolmasters monitored him constantly; ever afterward, he yearned for freedom. Rabindranath gave his first poetry recital at 14, and went to England with his older brother Satyendranath in 1878. After his return to **India** in 1880, Rabindranath experienced a beautiful spiritual vision, one that opened him more deeply to the beauty of life and the need to express that beauty through literature.

Rabindranath wrote poetry and plays on many subjects, but after 1900 his work became increasingly political. He pointed to India's degradation at the hands of the **British Empire**. In 1901, he began a school—a "Boys' Monastery"—which grew into the Visva-Bharati, or "World University." Tagore received the Nobel Prize for Literature in 1913; he was the first Asian to receive such an honor. The British Empire knighted him in 1913, but he renounced the honor in 1919.

Tagore traveled almost constantly in the last third of his life. He toured the United States, most of Europe, China, and Japan, and even accepted an offer to visit Mussolini's Italy. Along with **Mohandas Ghandi**, he was the most renowned Indian of his time.

Rabindranath and children

91. Tokugawa
Japanese rulers

In times of danger and turmoil in medieval Japan, one family—the Tokugawa—emerged to lead Japan into a serene, prosperous, and isolated period of more than 250 years.

Tokugawa Ieyasu (1543–1616) was born in Okazaki, Japan, a country that was rife with competing *daimyos* (feudal lords) and their combative samurai soldiers. As a child, Ieyasu was sent to a rival family as a hostage. He learned from his adversity and slowly built his

Tokugawa Ieyasu

own power base. By the early 1580s, he had become a daimyo and was associated with **Oda Nobunaga**, a fierce warrior who was attempting to bring all of Japan under his rule.

One of Nobunaga's men wounded him in 1582 and he committed suicide. Ieyasu was a logical contender to replace Nobunaga, but he ceded to another lord, Hideyoshi. While Hideyoshi embarked on ambitious military campaigns against Korea, Ieyasu built the fishing village of Edo into his fort, castle, and

headquarters; it later became the city of **Tokyo**.

Hideyoshi died in 1598. In 1600, Ieyasu won the critical Battle of Sekigahara against his a coalition of rival daimyos, and became the true master of Japan. The figurehead emperor formally named him *shogun* (military governor) in 1603. Ieyasu retired and gave the title to his son in 1605, but Ieyasu retained true power until his death 11 years later.

Tokugawa Hidetada (reigned 1605–32) followed many of his father's policies; most notably, he had four Christian missionaries executed in 1617. He also ruled that foreign trade vessels could enter Japan only at two places, Nagasaki and Hirado.

Son of Hidetada, **Tokugawa Iemitsu** (1604–1651), became shogun in 1623. Assured of his power, he eliminated the last few privileges of the emperor. Iemitsu expelled the last Christian missionaries and Portuguese merchants. Except for Dutch and Chinese ships that traded at Nagasaki, he closed Japan to the outside world. This isolationist policy determined Japanese history for the next 200 years.

Tokugawa Tsunayoshi (1646–1709), the fifth family shogun, became ruler in 1680. Japan enjoyed peace and prosperity during his rule.

From another branch of the family, Tokugawa Yoshimune (1684–1751) became the eighth shogun in 1716. He tried to return Japan to simplicity and austerity.

Tokugawa Yoshinobu (1837–1913) was the 15th and last Tokugawa shogun. He came to power in 1866, just as a revolt broke out. He surrendered his powers in 1867, fully believing that he would be first among the new rulers. Instead, the rebels began an imperial restoration, which led to the **Meiji** dynasty (see no. 69).

92. Tolstoy
Russian military leaders and writers

From peace to war, from czars to communism, the Tolstoy family has played an important role in Russian history.

The family story began in 1353, when Indris Tolstoy arrived in Russia from Lithuania. The country was then under **Mongol** rule, and Indris was welcomed as an aide to the Russians in their attempt to overthrow the foreign rulers.

Little is known of Indris's many descendants until 1642, when Andrei Tolstoy married Solominda Miloslavsky. Russian Czar Alexis's marriage to a member of the Miloslavsky clan in 1648 brought the Tolstoys close to the throne.

Their hopes for political position were stalled when Czar **Peter the Great**—Alexis's son from another marriage—took the throne in 1689. Brothers Ivan and Peter Tolstoy had to be careful around the Czar, who suspected their allegiance lay elsewhere. Peter eventually won the Czar's confidence, and in 1718 he followed Peter the Great's orders and had the heir to the throne, crown prince Alexei, killed in prison. For his loyalty, Czarina Catherine bestowed the title of count upon Peter Tolstoy before his death.

Alexander Osterman-Tolstoy rose to become an important military leader at the end of the 18th century. During Napoleon's march on Moscow, he commanded a Russian corps at the Battle of Borodino in 1812.

Feodor Ivanovich Tolstoy became known as "the American" of the family. He sailed

Count Leo Tolstoy

with the Russian Navy in 1803, and was marooned on an island off Russian Alaska. There he lived with the native Tlingits for more than a year before he was picked up by a ship and brought to Kamchatka in Russia. Tolstoy then crossed all of Siberia by foot, horse, and boat and reached home in 1805.

Aleksei Konstantinovich Tolstoy wrote historical and political plays. However, it was Count **Leo Tolstoy** (1828–1910) who left the deepest imprint on Russian society and world literature.

Leo was born at Yasnaya Polyana ("Bright Glade"), his family's estate in the Tula province. He served in the Russian army during the **Crimean War** and developed both a fascination with and repulsion to man's ability to kill other men. Tolstoy had a long and brilliant literary career, and is best remembered for his epic novel of Russian life during the Napoleonic wars—*War and Peace*—and the tragic story of adultery and the aristocracy, *Anna Karenina*.

During the last third of his life, Leo Tolstoy was plagued by a need to find spiritual meaning in life. His faith led him to denounce traditional religion, government, war, and private property.

Famed for their personal eccentricities and political astuteness, the ruling family of Tudors left a deep imprint on the history of England.

The English civil war between the Houses of Lancaster and York, known as the **Wars of the Roses** (1455–1485), took a great toll on the country's life and political stability. The solution to this misery came in the person of Henry, Duke of Richmond, who won the battle of Bosworth Field and assumed the throne as King **Henry VII** (reigned 1485–1509).

Henry married Elizabeth of York, daughter of Edward IV, to placate the Yorkist opposition. King Henry managed the royal finances with skill. He created the English navy, rebuilt the country's economy, and left a surplus in the treasury to his son, King **Henry VIII** (reigned 1509–1547) .

Strong, handsome, and highly intelligent, his subjects greatly preferred "King Hal" to his reclusive father. At first he governed well, but he was continually distracted by his need for a son and heir.

Married to Catherine of Aragon, the daughter of Ferdinand and Isabella of Spain, Henry wanted a divorce, since she had given birth to only a daughter, Mary. Pope Clement VII refused to grant a divorce; furious with the pope, Henry unilaterally broke away from Rome and created the **Church of England** with himself as its head. Then he granted himself a divorce.

Elizabeth I

Henry married, in succession, **Anne Boleyn** (whom he had executed), Jane Seymour (who died giving birth to their son, Edward), Anne of Cleves (whom he divorced), Catherine Howard (whom he had executed), and Catherine Parr (who had the good fortune to outlive the king). When he died, Henry left behind a disunited and nearly bankrupt kingdom.

Jane Seymour's son took the throne as King **Edward V** (reigned 1547–1553). He was succeeded by Queen Mary (reigned 1553–58), the daughter of Catherine of Aragon. Mary attempted to bring England back to the Catholic Church; she failed and her execution of 300 resisters created martyrs to the cause of the Church of England. Mary died in 1558, leaving the throne to Elizabeth, the daughter of Anne Boleyn.

Queen **Elizabeth I** (reigned 1558–1603) brought England and the Tudor dynasty back to glory. A clever stateswoman, she ran the kingdom with the same frugality and good sense that her grandfather Henry VII had. Although she steered a middle course between Catholicism and the new Church of England, when she died she left a kingdom that had taken irrevocable steps toward **Protestantism** Lacking an heir (she had never married), Elizabeth left the throne to her cousin, James VI of Scotland.

The family that ruled France during the late Middle Ages came from Valois, a county in northern France. The county was annexed to France in 1214 and French King Philip III gave the county to his younger son, Charles, in 1285.

Following the death of King Charles IV, last of the Capetian kings (see no. 21), the barons and churchmen of France gathered to select a new king. They bypassed the claim of English King Edward III, and chose Count Philip of Valois, who became King **Philip VI** (1293–1350) in 1328.

The selection led to neither harmony nor peace. England's Edward III began the Hundred Years' War with France to obtain what he believed to be his right to the throne. France saw very dark times; however, the Valois family continued to hold the throne. During the war, **Joan of Arc** helped save both the important city of Orléans and Crown Prince Charles by uniting the peasants in support of the Valois. The crown prince later became King **Charles VII** (reigned 1422–1461).

The crown was then passed down from father to son until the death of King Charles VIII (reigned 1483-1498). Charles left no male heir, so a related family branch, called Valois-Orléans, came to the throne. King Louis XII reigned from 1498 until 1515; he too left no successor, so the throne was passed to yet another branch, the Valois-Angouleme family.

Francis I (reigned 1515–1547) was a man of colossal and splendid appetites. During his reign, France blossomed with **Renaissance** art and architecture. Francis brought Leonardo da Vinci from Italy to work on massive artistic and engineering projects.

Francis I's son Henry II (reigned 1547–1559) married an Italian princess, Catherine de Médici. Henry died from a wound he received in a jousting tournament in 1559.

Queen Catherine presided as regent over the reigns of two of her sons, Francis II (reigned 1559–1560) and Charles IX (reigned 1560–1574). In 1572 Catherine persuaded her son Charles to attack the French Huguenots (Protestants) on St. Batholomew's Day. At least 12,000 **Huguenots** were killed in the "Bartholomew's Day Massacre" which prompted horror and outrage.

The massacre accelerated the religious warfare that nearly tore France to pieces. After Charles IX died, Catherine's last son became King **Henry III** (reigned 1574–1589). He fought a long and bloody war against the Catholic extremists led by Henry, Duke of Guise, and the Huguenots, led by Henry of Navarre. The war of the three Henrys finally ended when a religious fanatic stabbed Henry III to death. Prince Henry of Navarre converted to Catholicism and became the first **Bourbon** king of France.

Assassination of Henry III

Cornelius Vanderbilt

The name Vanderbilt is synonymous with great wealth in American business and investments.

Cornelius Vanderbilt (1794–1877) was born on Staten Island near New York City. The second son in his family, he had no childhood to speak of; from an early age he was directed to work. His father was a farmer and ferryman, and Cornelius directed his attention to the water surrounding Staten Island and nearby Manhattan Island. He worked in a ferry service and profited by filling the need for water transportation during the War of 1812. He married his first cousin, **Sophia Johnson**, and the couple had 13 children.

At the age of 26, Cornelius went to work for a steamboat owner. At the same time, his wife began to run a tavern in New Brunswick, New Jersey. The couple prospered, and in 1829 Vanderbilt began his own steamship line. His business soared, and in 1850 he inaugurated the first service to California by way of Nicaragua, instead of the traditional route by way of **Panama**. Cornelius turned to the railroad business very late in life, when he was 69. He acquired the New York and Harlem Railroad lines, then the Hudson River and New York Central lines. By the time of his death, he had extended train service all the way to Chicago.

William Henry Vanderbilt (1821–1885) received approximately 90 percent of the $100 million bequeathed to him by his father. (A sum of $4 million was divided among Vanderbilt's eight daughters.) William invested wisely, and at the time of his death, he left about $10 million to each of his eight children, thereby breaking a cardinal rule of his father, who had insisted the family fortune stay in one person's hands.

William Henry's sons Cornelius Vanderbilt II (1843–1899) and William Kissam (1849–1920) received control of the family's railroad interests. Cornelius II became head of the family. He and his wife built **The Breakers** at Newport, Rhode Island. This "summer cottage" of the Vanderbilt family was a huge, gaudy palace that seemed more appropriate for European than American tastes. William Kissam was an enthusiastic sportsman. He contributed to building and sailing the yacht *Defender*, which defeated an attempt by the British to win control of the **America's Cup,** the international sailing trophy.

Harold Stirling Vanderbilt (1884–1970), son of William Kissam, invented the game of contract bridge; he was also a noted yachtsman. Cornelius Vanderbilt III (1873–1942) was a railroad executive and a banker. His son, Cornelius Vanderbilt, Jr. (1898–1974), became a newspaperman and author.

96. Vasa
Swedish monarchs

The kings and queens of the Vasa dynasty brought Sweden to an era of greatness.

Gustavus Eriksson Vasa was a member of the Swedish nobility. In 1520, he led a national revolt against King Christian II of Denmark, who had tried to assert Danish supremacy over Sweden. In 1523, Vasa's fellow nobles elected him King of Sweden. As **Gustavus I** (reigned 1523–1560), he took advantage of the Lutheran Reformation begun by Martin Luther in 1517. The new king confiscated Roman Catholic property, and firmly allied his family with the new Lutheran cause.

The oldest of Gustavus's children, King Erik XIV (reigned 1560–1568) became mentally unstable during his reign, and the nobles officially deposed him in 1568.

Johan III (reigned 1568–1592) was the second of Gustavus's children. Initially popular, he lost the sympathies of his people when he began to favor Roman Catholicism.

Johan's son Sigismund was elected to the Polish throne in 1587. Sigismund also became king of Sweden after his father's death in 1592. His policies became quite unpopular, and the Swedish people deposed him in 1599. He remained king of Poland until his death in 1632.

Gustavus's youngest son, **Charles IX** (reigned 1604–1611), succeeded his nephew Sigismund. He fought a long war against Sigismund in Poland and contributed little to the development of Sweden as a European power. Charles's son, Gustavus II, better known as Gustavus Adolphus, came to the throne in 1611. He fought a series of wars that increased Swedish power and prestige, before his untimely death at the Battle of Breitenfeld in 1632.

Queen Christina (reigned 1632–1654) was Gustavus Adolphus's only child. During her reign, she became increasingly attracted to the Catholic faith. Tearfully, she abdicated the throne in 1654 to live as a true Catholic in Austria.

The third Vasa ruler after Christina was King **Charles XII** (reigned 1697–1718), who became famous as the most skillful and daring military leader of his day. During his reign, Charles fought a series of battles against Poland and Russia in the Great Northern War. Although Charles fought brilliantly, Czar **Peter the Great** of Russia eventually defeated him at the critical Battle of Poltava in 1709. By the time of Charles's death in 1718, Sweden had lost much of her wealth and power.

Queen **Ulrika Eleonora** (reigned 1718-1720) was the younger sister of King Charles XII. She ruled for only two years, then abdicated the throne in favor of her husband, Frederick (reigned 1720-1751). Ulrika died childless in 1741. That ended the direct Vasa line in Sweden.

Charles XII

A family descended from a duke of the House of Premysl ruled the kingdom of Bohemia for hundreds of years—and gave Christianity a strong foothold in a part of the Holy Roman Empire.

Bohemia (in the present-day Czech Republic), was part of the Holy Roman Empire in the ninth century A.D. Duke **Vratislav** (reigned A.D. 915–920) was the first member of the Premyslid dynasty in Bohemia. His son, Svaty Vaclav (Wenceslas in English), assumed power in Bohemia at the age of 15 in A.D. 922. Svaty Vaclav was a Christian, and during his seven years as duke, Christianity grew stronger in the kingdom.

In A.D. 929 Svaty Vaclav was murdered by his brother **Boleslav I** (reigned A.D. 929–67) inside the chapel of Boleslav's castle. Vaclav's tomb soon became a pilgrimage site for Christians; they reported that miraculous events took place there. Frightened by this, Boleslav had his brother's remains reinterred at the Church of St. Vitus in Prague. Svaty's fame as a holy person grew, and he became a great Bohemian hero. He was eventually declared St. Wenceslas and made the patron saint of **Czechoslovakia**.

Despite his crime, Boleslav became an effective duke of Bohemia. He helped the German Emperor, Otto I, defeat the Magyars and secured the eastern flank of Bohemia from attack. His son, **Bolesav II** (reigned A.D. 967–999), became known as Boleslav the Pious; by his death in A.D. 999, Bohemia had become a strong bastion of Christianity.

Otto I

The Premysl family continued to govern Bohemia until 1306. The family conquered nearby **Moravia** during the 11th century, and in 1085, Vratislav II (reigned 1061–1092) was crowned king, rather than duke, of Bohemia. The title was made hereditary in 1212, when the German emperor confirmed the rights of the Premysl family to hold the only crown other than his own in the Holy Roman Empire.

King **Ottokar I** (reigned 1198–1230) of Bohemia put his country on a path toward greatness that climaxed around the middle of the 13th century. His son, King **Wenceslas I** (reigned 1230–1253), brought Austria under his sway as well. His son, Ottokar II (reigned 1253–1278), led two crusades against the pagan Prussians and Lithuanians. By 1270 his realm extended from the Adriatic Sea to Silesia. Ottokar quarreled with German Emperor Rudolph Hapsburg and was defeated and killed in battle in 1278.

His son, King **Wenceslas II** (reigned 1278–1305), ruled Bohemia and briefly held power in Poland as well.

King Wenceslas III (reigned 1305–1306) was the last Premyslid king of Bohemia. He was assassinated as he was raising an army to cross the border into Poland and left no heir.

The Windsor line has brought the English monarchy into the 20th century with grace, but not without change.

In 1838, the 18-year-old **Alexandrina Victoria** (1819–1901) was crowned queen of England. She succeeded her uncle, William IV, last of the Hanoverian kings. Victoria married her German first cousin, Prince Albert of Saxe-Coburg-Gotha in 1840. Victoria and Albert formed one of the most loving and devoted royal couples in British history. Although Victoria held all the power, Albert played a wise and influential role in the development of British policy.

The couple had nine children: Victoria, Albert Edward (better known as "Bertie"), Alice, Alfred, Helena, Louise, Arthur, Leopold, and Beatrice. Through their marriages to members of other European royal families, Victoria became known as the "grandmother" of Europe.

The queen was inconsolable after Albert died of typhus in 1861. She abandoned her early, passionate approach to life and became a prim, conservative widow whose lifestyle gave birth to the name **Victorian Age**. Ironically, those 40 years were England's greatest period; Victoria became Empress of India as well as England's queen.

After Victoria's death in 1901, her son Albert Edward became King **Edward VII** (reigned 1901–1910). Witty, ironic, and rakish, he was already nearly 60 when he finally succeeded to the throne.

Edward was followed by his son, King **George V** (reigned 1910–1936), who held the throne as England entered World War I against Germany. In 1917, he officially changed the family name from Saxe-Coburg-Gotha to Windsor, to demonstrate his distance from his German royal relations.

George's eldest son, King **Edward VIII** (reigned 1936) was a charming, handsome man.

Elizabeth II and Philip

He abdicated the throne in December, 1936 to marry Wallis Simpson, an American divorcee.

His brother, King **George VI** (reigned 1937–1952) succeeded him. A shy man, he was complimented by his outgoing, dynamic wife, Elizabeth. George's daughter, Queen **Elizabeth II** (b. 1926), came to the throne in 1952. Before her succession to the throne, Elizabeth married Prince Philip, Lord Mountbatten, and they had four children: Charles, Anne, Andrew, and Edward.

The lives of Elizabeth's children have brought tragedy and a degree of scandal to Britain's royal family. Prince Charles married Lady Diana Spencer in 1981, but they had a troubled marriage that ended in divorce in 1996. After the divorce, Diana remained immensely popular around the world, and her death in a car accident in 1997 left millions of people in mourning. Prince Andrew married Sarah Ferguson in 1986, but their marriage was also troubled. They divorced in 1994.

During the turbulent 15th century in England, the House of York reigned, yet its members spent many years in bloody disputes trying to secure their right to rule.

Edmund of Langley (1341–1402) was the first duke of York; he received the title from his nephew, King **Richard II**, in 1385. The second duke was Edmund's eldest son, Edward Plantagenet. A gallant knight, Edward was crushed to death at Agincourt, one of the key battles of the long Hundred Years' War between England and France.

Richard Plantagenet (1411–1460) was a grandson of Edmund of Langley. He chose his surname to emphasize his descent from the Plantagenet dynasty (see no. 76) of England. By this time, the Plantagenents had been replaced by the House of Lancaster, which had taken the throne of England in 1400.

In 1450, with the hope of regaining the English throne, Richard Plantagenet started the dynastic struggle that became known as the **Wars of the Roses.** During the long wars, the House of York used the white rose as its symbol. The Lancasters chose the red rose. The Yorkists triumphed in 1460. Duke Richard's right to the throne was acknowledged, but he died at the Battle of Wakefield later that same year.

Richard Plantagenet's eldest son became King **Edward IV** in 1461. His reign was interrupted by the continuing struggles between the two houses of York and Lancaster. He reigned until 1470, and then again from 1471 until his death in 1483. King Edward's eldest son succeeded him as King Edward V, but he reigned for less than a year. He and his younger brother, Richard Plantagenet, are known in English history as the **"Princes in the Tower."** Their uncle, King Richard III (reigned 1483–1485), had usurped the throne and imprisoned them in the Tower of London.

Richard III, the last Yorkist king, was defeated and killed at the **Battle of Bosworth Field** in 1485. The English crown went to Duke Henry of Richmond, who established the new Tudor dynasty (see no. 93). King **Henry VII** (reigned 1485-1509) reconciled the two families through his marriage to Elizabeth, eldest daughter of the Yorkist King Edward IV.

Edward IV

Before his death in 1483, King Edward IV gave his second son the title of the duke of York. Since that time the second son of English monarch—second in line to the throne after the Prince of Wales—has traditionally held this title.

100. Zrínyi
Croatian military leaders

Since Croatia became an independent nation during the 1990s, there has been a revival of interest in its history and people. For nearly 200 years, the Zrínyi family played a key role in that history.

Since 1102, Croatia and Hungary had been separate countries ruled by the same monarch. King **Louis II** (reigned 1516–1526) was the last king to rule all of Hungary before

Suleiman besieging Vienna

its conquest by the Turks. At the Battle of Mohács in 1526, King Louis was defeated and killed by the victorious Ottoman Turks. The Hapsburg family of Vienna then claimed to be the new ruling family for both Hungary and Croatia; the Croatian nobles agreed, and elected King Ferdinand as their new monarch.

Croatian **Miklós Zrínyi** (1508–1566) distinguished himself at the siege of Vienna in 1529. This Hapsburg victory prevented the Ottoman Sultan, **Suleiman the Magnificent**, from entering central Europe. For his military service, Ferdinand named Zrínyi ban (viceroy) of Croatia.

Zrínyi's military exploits in behalf of the Hapsburgs earned him the bitter hatred of

Suleiman. In 1566, Suleiman brought 100,000 Turkish troops to Croatia and besieged Zrínyi at the castle of **Sziget**. Zrínyi, who had 2,500 soldiers, responded to the Turkish siege with great bravado, which only further infuriated the sultan.

The siege began on August 5 and lasted until September 8; then Zrínyi and his remaining soldiers made a last charge over the ramparts and the dead bodies of their comrades and thousands of fallen Turks. Zrínyi and all his followers were killed. However, Suleiman did not live to see the castle taken; he had died in his tent on the night of September 5. Having suffered thousands of casualties, the Turks withdrew, leaving Zrínyi and his men as martyrs to the cause of Croatian freedom.

Zrínyi's family line continued, and his great-grandson, **Miklós Zrínyi** (1620–1664), became ban of **Croatia** in 1647. An outstanding military leader who defeated the Turks several times, he wanted to expel both the Turks and the Hapsburg rulers.

Miklós was also a man of literary distinction. He wrote *The Peril of Sziget* in honor of his great-grandfather, and was one of the first writers to use Hungarian as a literary language.

Peter Zrínyi (1621–1671) was Miklós's younger brother. He became ban of Croatia in 1665. Peter conspired against Hapsburg Emperor Leopold I, and when his plans were uncovered, he was executed. His daughter Helen Zrínyi married Francis I Rakoczy, the prince of Transylvania. Their son Francis II (1676–1735) died while fighting against the Hapsburgs. For his heroism, he became a national hero of Hungary.

TRIVIA QUIZ & PROJECTS

Test you knowledge and challenge your friends with the following questions. The answers are contained in the biographies noted.

1. Which American family produced two of the first six United States presidents? (see no. 2)

2. What ocean tragedy took the life of a prominent real estate tycoon? (see no. 3)

3. Who was the 19th century American actor who temporarily retired from the stage because of the murderous actions of his younger brother? (see no. 11)

4. Which British prime minister was descended from a long line of English dukes, but whose mother was an American-born heiress? (see no. 25)

5. Where did a famous English scientist find surprising evidence that led him to produce his theory than humans probably descended from apes? (see no. 28)

6. Which actor won an Academy Award in a 1981 movie for playing the father of his real-life daughter? (see no. 35)

7. How did a movie actress born in Philadelphia wind up becoming one of Europe's most famous princesses? (see no. 42)

8. Who is the only American to be both the son of one U.S. president and the father of another? (see no. 49)

9. Why did the 20th century reign of the Hohenzollern Dynasty's Wilhelm II turn out to be a disaster? (see no. 50)

10. Which family was the official court painters for nearly 200 years for the Tokugawa shoguns, the military commanders who ruled Japan? (see no. 55)

11. Who are the husband-and-wife team of English scientists who proved that human life first evolved in Africa? (see no. 60)

12. Why did a powerful Aztec leader allow an army of Spanish conquerors to enter his city without putting up any resistance? (see. no. 72)

13. Where did a family of Italian merchants travel to during the 13th century that no other European had traveled to before ? (see no. 78)

14. What military decision by a Russian czar forced his eventual abdication from the throne and led to a revolution in his country? (see no. 81)

15. How did Napoleon's defeat at the battle of Waterloo lead to the enrichment of a family of European bankers? (see no. 83)

16. Why did a 16th century English monarch break away from the Roman Catholic Church and create his own Church of England? (see no. 93)

Suggested Projects

1. Choose two families from this book with the same backgrounds or occupations— e.g. political leaders, monarchs, financiers, actors, etc. Write a fictional diary entry for one member of each of the two families that describes in detail one of the most significant days in each of their lives. Then write one or two paragraphs describing how these two people are alike and how they are different.

2. Write a brief history of your own family. Begin with the story of how your ancestors first came to this country. (If you know the details of their arrival; if not, start with any information you have about the lives of the earliest generations of your family.) In addition to writing about your grandparents, parents, and siblings, make sure you include information about other relatives, such as aunts, uncles, cousins, and in-laws. When you've completed your history, create a family tree; include names and years of births and deaths, if you know them.

Index

Index

Index

Index